Invisible *to* INVINCIBLE!

The Mindset and Tools to Monetise your Passion using Facebook and Live Events for Business

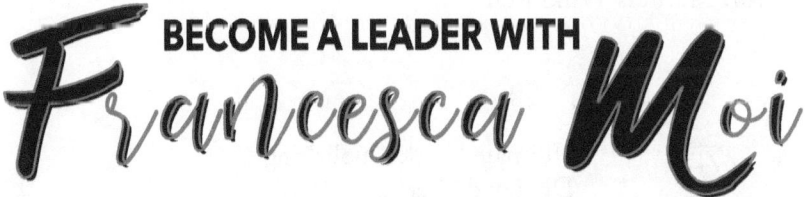

BECOME A LEADER WITH Francesca Moi

First published by Ultimate World Publishing 2020
Copyright © 2020 Francesca Moi

ISBN

Paperback - 978-1-922372-32-1
Ebook - 978-1-922372-33-8

Francesca Moi has asserted her right under the Copyright, Designs and Patents Act 1988 to be identified as the author of this work. The information in this book is based on the author's experiences and opinions. The publisher specifically disclaims responsibility for any adverse consequences, which may result from use of the information contained herein. Permission to use information has been sought by the author. Any breaches will be rectified in further editions of the book.

All rights reserved. No part of this publication may be reproduced, stored in or introduced into a retrieval system, or transmitted in any form, or by any means (electronic, mechanical, photocopying, recording or otherwise) without the prior written permission of the author. Any person who does any unauthorised act in relation to this publication may be liable to criminal prosecution and civil claims for damages. Enquiries should be made through the publisher.

Cover design: Ultimate World Publishing
Layout and typesetting: Ultimate World Publishing
Editor: Marinda Wilkinson

Ultimate World Publishing
Diamond Creek,
Victoria Australia 3089
www.writeabook.com.au

ACKNOWLEDGEMENTS

A super huge thank you to Natasa and Stuart Denman for publishing this book and believing in me from my first book *Follow Me – Shuuttup and build your network*.

They have been such a huge inspiration and example for me in life and business.

Thank you to my family, my mum Adriana that is my rock. She is always there for me and supports all my decisions. My dad Antonello who went from the biggest skeptic to becoming my biggest raving fan. To my brother Patrizio who is an example of what is possible when you don't give up!

To all my clients who have believed in my services and products, they have made my dreams come true!

To all the 'Marias' who have been following me and downloading all my stuff for free and never pay me any money! Without them I wouldn't be here! #grateful

To my team who have been coming along for the ride, and what a ride! They have added so much value and ideas to wow our clients every day. I wanted to offer a special thank you to my team that have joined me on this journey and a special shout out to the following contributors to this book:

- Jenny
- Tina
- Bebs
- Elizabeth
- Aimee

Thank you from the bottom of my heart!

To the universe that always has my back.
To grace that is in my heart every moment of every day.

To faith that is the force of my life.

TESTIMONIALS

Francesca Moi has learned the secret of passion and how not to follow the money. Follow your passions, which leads to greater prosperity and fulfillment! Fantastic read, with real examples for real people.

William Farmer, Managing Director
Dale Carnegie Australia

As an entrepreneur who was invisible, this book has given me practical tools, steps and strategies to implement immediately. As a result of the concepts shared in this book, my family business has rapidly transformed from being a 'hobby' to moving towards a successful six-figure business. As a mum with two children and a fly in fly out husband, if I can do it so can YOU!

Francesca has a superpower, communicating complicated theories and strategies and breaking them down to bite-sized, practical steps which will have you moving towards the life and business of your dreams from the moment you read or hear them.

A talented and gifted businesswomen Francesca shares from her heart her own personal story which makes it easy to connect with and understand that her success is a result of a constant commitment to her MINDSET. This book is a great companion for any business owner wanting more out of their life and business.

Immersing yourself in this book will do more than just improve your business. It is a holistic approach to improving all areas of your life. If you are ready to RISE UP and live your best life,

READ THIS BOOK, DO THE EXERCISES, DREAM BIG and DONT MAKE EXCUSES!

It changed my life and my family's life, so what are you waiting for GET TO IT!

Diane Mckendrick, Author, Speaker, Life coach, CEO
www.dianemckendrick.com

Francesca writes with such passion and authenticity that it is easy to get lost in the pages. Her honesty and vulnerability are evident as she shares her journey of how she turned her life around from self-sabotaging and wanting to hide, to a woman who is a motivated, passionate action taker. By way of implementing practical steps, she helps you to break through your limiting beliefs and to step out of your comfort zone to find your passion and live life on your terms. Francesca is definitely a woman who walks her talk and she will teach you to do the same.

Alison Felton
www.helixnutrition@bigpond.com

Testimonials

This book helped me realise that it's okay to be me! By focusing on the positive and the things I CAN do (rather than the things I'm not good at), it frees up more time and energy to give to myself and to others. I can make more of an impact on the world by sharing my true self. Francesca has also taught me the importance of connection and passion. By 'just being me' I am able to authentically connect with my family, my friends and my network. This has helped me in all aspects of life: family, friendship and business. In reading this book, you will discover what lights your fire and what you are truly passionate about. Never give up, and never be afraid to try! You just might surprise yourself with how much you can achieve.

Jamie McVeigh
www.intellikidsystems.com

I've only just started reading this book and I'm already excited about the possibilities. It's helped me reflect on how I used to think and whether I'm still holding onto some of those patterns. I feel inspired, motivated and ready to take action!!

Elizabeth Elenor, The Spiritual Warrior
www.elizabethelenor.com

All Francesca's books are informative, helpful and jam-packed with tools to help you succeed. However, this book comes from deep within her heart, to help people find their purpose and passion! The best leaders in the world take their people on the journey WITH them and FM's book does exactly that – it is vulnerable, honest and conveys how you can get what you want in life. I love the questions at the end of each chapter that force you to think, I had 'aha' moments with every one. LIFE changing! Thanks so much FM, you continue to inspire me every day.

Nicolette Jane

What a great insight into the journey that is responsible for the force of nature that is Francesca Moi. FM has such a passion and enthusiasm for helping people to live their lives on purpose, doing what they love and her inspirational mindset is contagious. I am grateful to have her as my coach, mentor and friend and one of the best things about her guidance is that she believes in you even when you may be beginning to have your doubts. I would recommend this book to anyone who has ever lacked self-belief and is wanting to take the plunge into a life filled with passion, power and purpose. Well done Francesca, as expected pure authenticity, passion and grace.

Sam Bowker
www.happyuhq.com.au

CONTENTS

Acknowledgements	iii
Testimonials	v
Introduction	1
Chapter 1: Mindset from Invisible to Invincible	3
Chapter 2: Finding Your Purpose and Passion	17
Chapter 3: Failing Your Way to Success	29
Chapter 4: Invisible to Invincible in My Life	45
Chapter 5: Your Business from Invisible to Invincible	59
Chapter 6: Invisible to Active	79
Chapter 7: Active to Established	91
Chapter 8: Established to Empowered	103
Chapter 9: Empowered to Invincible	115
Chapter 10: Stay Invincible	127
Chapter 11: Stay Centred and Get Rid of Ego	139
Chapter 12: Grow A Culture and A Legacy	155
Afterword	167
About the Author	169
Hire a VA	173

INTRODUCTION

As I write this introduction, I find it difficult to find the words to describe how fortunate I feel to have written my third book. Although this book has taken me much longer than the first two (about eight months longer!), I have enjoyed writing it the most as I have reflected on how far I've grown as a person and business owner.

It has taken me most of my life to find my true passion, and the moment I figured out what it was, was when the real Francesca Moi was born. I was put on this planet to help others make their dreams come true, so that together we can create positive ripples across the world for years to come. I truly love waking up every morning with the goal to encourage everyone around me to help others and achieve success.

Like most entrepreneurs, my business wasn't built overnight. I have spent countless hours and many sleepless nights building the community I have now. I had to believe that I was worthy to invest in myself to make my dreams come true. I had to put in the time, the money and the effort to achieve everything I have today.

I'm not saying the hard work is over; far from it. I still wake up every morning and roll my sleeves up, ready for the next stage of my journey. I don't know when the end of my journey will be – I like to think there is no end. I like to think that every day I wake up with the mindset that I can always grow and learn, and if I can learn something new every day then my journey will never be over.

I continue to grow my community of over 350 business owners and entrepreneurs, who all have the same vision and determination as me. It is quite amazing we have been able to come together to lift each other up and raise the vibrations on this planet. Every single member of my Academy Family has been able to use my strategies to step up and achieve success in their niche.

I am hoping this book finds its way to the next Francesca Moi – the next person who is trying to find their passion in this life. The next person who wants to make a difference. The next person who wants to work as hard as they can to make all their dreams come true. I hope this book finds its way to the next person who is just about to give up. I hope this book proves to them they can make their dreams come true. And I hope they use my strategies to get to the next level. To go from invisible to invincible.

CHAPTER 1

MINDSET FROM INVISIBLE TO INVINCIBLE

'Your business is a 3D printout of your thoughts.'
– Francesca Moi

When I was little, my dad was always very busy at work. He would leave early and come home late and I always wanted to spend more time with him. I remember when I was four years old fighting with my brother over who would get to spend Sunday mornings with him.

One Sunday morning in December, I woke up early and it was freezing. It was so cold, I thought it was going to snow in the house. It was silent, so I thought I was the first one up! *YAY! I get to spend time with Daddy!* I thought my brother was still sleeping but as I went downstairs, I found my dad with my brother at the piano ready to start playing together.

So, I decided to lie to get Dad's attention:

'I would love to learn how to play piano, Daddy.' He always wanted my brother and I to be interested in music and he couldn't believe his dream finally came true when those words came out of my mouth. I would have said anything to make him happy, even a lie. He really wanted me to be a pianist like my brother.

My dad pushed my brother aside and asked me to show him how I played. I thought just banging my hands on the piano would do it. But no way!

What a DISASTER!

While I attempted to play the piano, my dad said, *'Franci, leave it, you are not as talented as your brother. Never bang the piano this way again!'*

At the time, it was devastating. This moment was defining for me because it made me believe I wasn't good enough. Not as good as my brother. That I would never achieve anything, that I shouldn't even try. It made me go into ego and into fear of failing. And to avoid failure, I started to avoid everything.

I now know if you're not passionate about something, you're not going to be fulfilled. I am glad I didn't keep trying to be a pianist because it's not what I truly wanted to be.

There was also a time when my mum once encouraged me to join a classic dancing class. I hated it! And because I didn't want to do it, I started hurting myself. I would do cartwheels and get stuck with my neck against the wall. And by the time my mum would come pick me up, she'd find me in the corner, stuck with my head on the floor and couldn't walk. She would ask the teacher, *'Why is my daughter in the corner?'*. This happened almost every time, so eventually Mum felt sorry for me and pulled me out of the class.

I felt I was winning every time. I got pulled out of a class I didn't want to be a part of, so this caused me to find excuses about anything. I became a really good excuse maker and not an action taker for many, many years.

From that point on, I was making excuses all the time. I stopped learning anything new, stopped trying new things and eventually began pretty much failing at everything. It became a pattern for me.

One time I went to play volleyball, and I didn't want to do it. I didn't want to play in a group because I didn't want to stand out. I didn't want to fail. I didn't want to look stupid in front of everybody. And when you are afraid of something, you usually manifest your fears.

I will never forget, it was game time, my mum was in the audience with the other parents, but my dad wasn't there. He knew I was going to embarrass him so he preferred to not show up. Actually, that is what I told myself at the time, but he was probably just busy working like always.

The other team was so strong, I tried to avoid touching the ball, but the other team saw I was the weakest player of my team, so they started to hit the ball towards me to score. One of these balls hit me straight on my nose. I was bleeding and obviously Mum felt sorry for me, so she pulled me out. YAY!!! I mean, I was devastated and embarrassed but at least I achieved my goal of being pulled out of class.

Everything I was doing only made me a better excuse maker and not an action taker. I've since realised that I was afraid of standing out, I was afraid of playing in groups, I was afraid of looking silly or stupid because I didn't think I was good enough. I believed my brother was better than me. I let this limiting belief hold me back for years. I didn't believe in myself; I didn't believe that I could be successful. I didn't believe I was going to do anything with my life.

My brother always got help and support from my mum. Every afternoon she would help him with his homework. So, when I started going to school, I thought, great, I'm going to spend every afternoon with Mum doing homework instead of being by myself. When I started school, the teacher told my mum that I was super smart and already knew how to read and write, so I didn't need any extra support. Mum was relieved, thinking, *Thank goodness I just have to look after my Patrizio and not Francesca.* So, she didn't let me do my homework with them.

I felt left out.

So, guess what? I sabotaged it!

I stopped reading, I stopped doing homework, I stopped studying. I wanted to get attention by not being good at school. However, this still didn't work because Mum believed what the teacher said and kept repeating to me, *'You're clever! Come on, just do it!'* and she wouldn't help me. This was so frustrating to me because I was desperately wanting them to notice me. I've always felt that my brother was the one who was noticed and helped first, in everything!

What I didn't know at the time was that they were believing in me. They knew I had massive potential and I just couldn't see it. The love was there, the love is always there. But sometimes, if we don't see it delivered the way we expect it, we assume it is not there.

So, I grew up into a very shy, very insecure little girl who was really looking for Dad's love and approval.

When I was about 10 years old, something shocking happened in my family. One of our family members attempted suicide. It was devastating. Luckily, she was saved and didn't manage to kill herself. My dad showed so much love and compassion for this person, that as a 10-year-old I came to the conclusion that the only way to get Dad's love is to be suicidal like her. I began to write in my journal about how I was wishing something bad would happen to me. I was literally writing things like, *'I want to die*' and '*I hope something happens to me*'. I wanted to get noticed and get extra love from my dad.

One of the things I'm most passionate about now, is helping kids who are having these kinds of thoughts. So many people I have spoken to since have had suicidal thoughts or have thought at least once, '*maybe it would be easier if I die*'. I really want to help others and change the world, because there is a way for people to stop running away from the truth and look deeper inside.

My dad had always loved me. I just couldn't see it.

We have all been there. We have listened to that little voice in our head telling us we aren't good enough. We need to stop that voice now and start to work on our mindset. As I said in the opening quote, I believe our life is a 3D printout of our thoughts. Our bodies are a 3D printout of our thoughts. If we have these really bad thoughts, we're going to start putting on weight, or losing too much weight, as our self-worth is low. Your body is going to look like a 3D printout of your thoughts. The same thing happens in business and the same happens in our life.

To be safe, I told myself I had to avoid failure. That was my truth.

But what is yours?

Awareness is everything

Do you find your negative thoughts are being manifested in your life and when your life is falling apart, you don't know how to start to make it better?

I turned my life around and you can too. You can start the work by using the tips I'm going to share with you on how I went from wanting to be invisible, wanting to hide, wanting to die, wanting to disappear – to building a million-dollar business in four years on the other side of the world. All by myself.

You need to be aware of your thoughts in order to understand yourself. Once you realise how these thoughts are affecting or impacting your day, you will start to understand yourself on a deeper level and have more clarity around what is going on in your life. Furthermore, being able to explore why you are having these thoughts to begin with, will take your understanding to the next level. Be kind with yourself and start with awareness.

Find yourself a coach

When I found myself a coach back in 2013, I was able to start to look inside. At the time I was sabotaging myself a lot and I wasn't willing to go really deep into my thoughts. I found myself picking and choosing what I wanted to work on. But my very first coach did not let me play small and he asked me the following two questions:

What is your goal in life?

What do you want out of life?

And I was like, I don't know? I have no idea how to answer these questions!

He kept asking questions and going deeper to see where all my limiting beliefs came from. He was asking questions about my family, questions about my brother and questions about almost everything. He understood that all the failures that were happening now and had happened in the past, were all attached to how I perceived my family and relationships.

Surround yourself with people who inspire

I started to go to workshops, courses and seminars where there was a lot of people who were willing to grow and learn. They wanted to take their business, life and themselves to the next level. The best investment is having a supportive community around you who will help you grow! I finally decided to start looking inside and start growing and start learning.

When you are surrounded by people who are keen to grow alongside you, you will feel motivated to keep growing and not stay steady. You can openly share stories about your childhood and share the limiting beliefs you had. That's when you start to find the truth about your stories.

For example, I grew up believing that being a failure at piano meant I wasn't talented in anything.

That wasn't the truth at all, the truth was the opposite, the truth is always the opposite of what our ego says to us in our heads. The truth was, that I just wasn't talented in piano. So what? There were other things I could have explored to find my passion, instead of taking that as an absolute truth.

Let go of limiting beliefs

It's very simple: our ego is always trying to protect us and in doing so, most of the time, it limits us. And when that happens, we just go straight into a block and we build a wall that we won't let anyone break. The truth about me failing at everything is that I was manifesting it. I was doing it. I wanted to get hurt in volleyball; I wanted to get hurt at dancing. I was trying so desperately to avoid failure.

At times we want to be right so badly that we make things go wrong so we can be right. A friend of mine always thought people were avoiding her, so her ego made her protect herself by being grumpy all the time. Then, because she was always grumpy, people started to avoid her and she could finally say, 'See I was right believing that everybody avoids me. I am always alone'.

But, she didn't realise that it was her attitude that everyone was avoiding. When she finally understood she could change her truth at any time, her attitude began to change, and people didn't avoid her anymore.

We create our own reality.

We all have a choice.

What voice are you choosing? What thought are you believing to be true?

I thought my dad would love me more if I was unwell or suicidal. I believed my dad would love me more if I died. This was so far from the truth because this would have caused immense pain and heartbreak. And in fact, the only thing that stopped me from following through with those stupid thoughts was when I was writing a letter to them. I began feeling guilty because I knew I was going to create so much pain. I would have made them suffer – my brother, Mum and Dad. Why would I do that to them?

We are all loved; a human being wouldn't survive the first few months of its life without love. So, let's see it, feel it and hear it. Love is everywhere if you are willing to see it.

Have you ever asked yourself…

What if you don't live your purpose?

What if you live your life, and then at the end, you have all these regrets? For example, *I should have done more to discover my purpose and live by it,* or *I shouldn't have listened to those limiting beliefs*. What if you had a purpose to change people's lives and you suddenly realise you haven't followed through? That you just wasted your life without making any impact whatsoever? Without changing people's lives, without making a difference. The moment I recognised that I really wanted to do something with my life was when I thought to myself, *Hold on a second there is more to life, you don't need to just go to job that you hate, and hang out with people who are negative, and just whine about life and eat and feel sad. There's so much more to it!*

So, what if you don't follow your purpose? What if you don't listen to your mission? What will happen to your life? If you do that, would you have any regrets?

Ask yourself the opposite question. Always remember the opposite of what your ego says is the truth.

What if you settle for small or average?

It's never too late to make a change. For most of my life I have settled. I was working in an office, doing a really good job and the boss asked me if I was interested in applying for a promotion. I said NO WAY! Why? I didn't want to become a supervisor or manager because I was afraid. What if it was too hard? Too much work? Or what if I failed? My decisions used to be based on keeping it low-key and average so I didn't stand out. So that I couldn't fail. If you aren't taking action, there is no way to fail – only people that act can fail.

I was a smoker for most of my life because I didn't want to be perfect and I wanted to blend in with everyone. In Italy everybody smokes. Well, not everybody but a lot of people smoke and I didn't want to be any different. I wanted to be like everybody else. I would rather smoke and die of cancer than be different from everyone else. When I first got to Australia and started to work on my mindset and the business started to take off, people started to put me on a pedestal so I decided to keep smoking and overeating so I could show them how NOT PERFECT I was. I didn't want to feel 'too successful' and I could say to people, 'I smoke and overeat, see? I am not perfect, you can be my friend'.

Our mind will do anything for instant pleasure to avoid pain, without recognising the long-term pain it creates for us.

You will never feel fulfilled if you don't push out of your comfort zone and strive to be more than average.

What if you allow others to hold you back?

I have allowed others, and especially my own ego, to hold me back. I've let the things around me hold me back, to stop me from achieving my full potential. Then one day, I recognised that the only thing holding me back were all the thoughts in my head and I could actually achieve everything I want – and you can too!

If you don't step outside your comfort zone you might not be the example you want to be to your kids and you may not leave a legacy. If you hold yourself back or let other people hold you back, you won't achieve your purpose, mission and everything you want in this life. Take a look at those in your life and think about who is currently holding you back. Then look at what thoughts are holding you back. Maybe you don't realise what your purpose is yet – but you do know that you want to make a difference. What is stopping you from achieving that?

At the end of every chapter I will give you three actions to take. These are the action steps that will make change happen. Remember, I learned to be an ACTION TAKER and not an excuse maker, and this mindset shift changed everything. So, go ahead… take action!

The three actions you're going to take from this chapter are:

1. Answer the following questions in the space below or in your notebook or journal. Where are you trying to be invisible in your life? What areas in your life are you trying to be invisible? Is it love? Is it family? Is it friendship? Is it your business or a job? What is the area in your life you are trying to not achieve too much in, because there's a risk of failing or a fear of failure?

_____
_____
_____
_____
_____
_____

2. Write down why you're trying to be invisible. What are you trying to avoid? What is the why? What is the feeling you don't want to feel?

_____
_____
_____
_____
_____
_____
_____

3. What would happen if you were invincible? What does an invincible mindset look like in other areas in your life? In life, in business, in friendships, in love? What would that feel like? Write it down so you can begin to act on it.

_____
_____
_____
_____
_____
_____
_____

CHAPTER 2

FINDING YOUR PURPOSE AND PASSION

'Life doesn't happen to you, it happens for you!'
Tony Robbins

I know, I know there is so much pressure around this topic. What is your passion? What is your purpose?

I grew up thinking I didn't have a passion. I grew up thinking I wasn't special enough to deserve to have a passion or a talent for that matter. I didn't think I deserved it. I kept comparing myself to my brother, who is an extremely talented pianist and musician. Every time he touched the piano, he would create magic.

So, in comparison to him, who am I?

'I have no passion. I am a nobody and never will be somebody.'

I had this reoccurring thought to just give up, which echoed in my head throughout my life, ever since I was a teenager. I just thought I had to give up. I don't have a passion. Not everybody has a passion. That's what I used to think.

But guess what? That is not true! Everybody has a passion deep inside, they just have to find it. I was lucky enough to find my passion at the age of 31. Better late than never!

My mum always loved healing and card reading, but never thought she was any good at it. Then, at the age of 65, she started a very successful business healing others and helping people love themselves. So yes, it's most definitely never too late!

Everybody deserves to find their passion and you do too. If you do have a passion, then you're going to love this chapter because it's going to confirm what drives you in this life. If you don't – strap yourself in and let's do this!

When you discover your passion, you have a reason to wake up every morning. I used to wake up every morning and just feel useless. I didn't have a purpose, I didn't have a mission and didn't have anything to look forward to. I felt I didn't have anybody that needed me. I didn't have anybody to impact or make a difference to change their life. Living just for you is the most selfish and sad way to live life because in this life, we're not here for us. We're here to help. We're here to contribute. We're here to give. We're here to love. Waking up every day just for you is not enough to feel the passion and be happy. When was the last time you jumped out of bed feeling happy and excited about life? I do that most days now because I know my purpose. I'm on a mission. I know what I'm doing and know that everything is coming together and everything is meant to be.

Discovering your passion

Where does passion come from and what exactly is it? Think about that. It's a feeling, an emotion, but how can you recognise it and where can you find it? Where do you feel it and what does it feel like? How do you know you are feeling it?

When you search in the dictionary, passion is defined as a, 'strong and barely controllable emotion'.

Emotion comes from your mind. Passion and purpose don't come from external sources, they come from within. Passion is not something that happens to us. We choose it every day. I choose every day to live in a passionate state, I choose every day to be a passionate woman in my business, I choose the way I feel. It doesn't happen to me: I make it happen.

I used to look at happy people and wonder how come they were so happy all the time and I felt so lost inside.

Until I realised they choose to feel happy. Now I choose to be happy – and you can too!

Why am I here? That was the question that kept popping into my head. There must be more to life. At one point, after years of living and surviving, I truly started to ask myself important questions like: why am I here? What is my purpose in this lifetime? What is that I need to be doing to feel fulfilled? There must be more to life, than having a job I hate, getting home after work, cooking dinner and watching TV. There must be more to life and what is it all about?

Well, when I was making my life ALL ABOUT ME, I couldn't see it. I couldn't find the answers to all these questions.

I couldn't see that giving back and contributing to other people's lives was going to make me feel alive. I now know we need to help, support and give to feel alive and fulfilled. In the last few years, I have realised that even having a successful million-dollar business is not going to make me feel happy. The happiness comes with the contribution. It's all about giving. It's all about supporting others! It's all about putting yourself out there and making a difference, making an impact.

I believe that every single one of us has a passion. We all have a passion! The passion doesn't need to be the same all your life either. It can change. Passion is that burning desire that wakes you up every day and makes you go and do what makes you truly happy. If your passion lies within the health industry, you may be excited to wake up and cook something healthy to fuel your body or to focus on nutrition and exercise. I bet you go to the gym. If your passion is to help others, from the moment you wake up you are looking for ways to help. You never put yourself first. If your passion is business, you wake up and the first thing you want to do is grab your phone and check your social media and emails because that's what you're passionate about.

When you are passionate, you can't wait. It means being obsessed with something that gives you a buzz. It gives you something to look forward to, it gives you the butterfly feeling in the stomach that gets you super excited. When you get the feeling, go deeper and keep asking yourself why. Why is this your passion? Why do you want to do this? What is the meaning behind that? Why are you passionate about business? The more you dig, the more you will find that it's all connected. Look closely at the feelings attached to it – it could be love, clarity, gratefulness or the feeling of being useful. It's not just about the thing you are passionate about, it's also about the feeling you get when you follow your passion. Everything we do, every action we take is generated by a feeling and if you are not passionate enough you are going to struggle to act, grow and find your purpose.

Your purpose is the why

To me, purpose and passion go together. Purpose is the *why* you are passionate about something. Passion is the *doing* of it. Passion is the butterfly, the adrenaline, the endorphin that comes into your brain. To be successful at something we need to find an obsession – and obsession comes with passion.

When talking to other successful business owners, I always ask them: are you obsessed with your business? And they always say, 'Yes! I couldn't do what I do if I didn't have the obsession'.

Those who are in business only for money, only to make money, will end up being bored and will eventually want to stop. So, you need to find that passion, the thing that ignites the obsession in you. I spend a lot of time studying successful business owners and entrepreneurs, people who are making a difference, and they all have one thing in common: they have an addictive personality. When they find something they love, they just devour it because they just can't stop. And as long as it's healthy for you, that's what you want. You want to get so obsessed that all you can think about is that one thing. At least until you have gained momentum.

Getting obsessed when you want to get good at something means putting your absolute all into achieving success. Everybody that has achieved success has, at some point, been obsessed by it.

It's all about making things happen and pushing yourself to be the best version of you. I believe that whenever we want to succeed, we have to do things that other people don't do. I am always thinking how I can go above and beyond compared to the person sitting next to me. I always try and be ahead of them. While they're sleeping, I'm working.

When you are striving to achieve something, get obsessed with working on yourself first and then focus on your business and use your obsession to take it to the next level. Once I master something and it eventually becomes subconscious, then I keep focusing on it and doing it. Then I bring something new into it and it's like bringing magic.

Some people may look at obsession as a negative connotation or concept, but to me, it's more of an alignment with being congruent to what I really believe and the way that I focus on visualising things, experiencing things in my mind before I experience them in reality.

I know if I visualise what I want, it will happen or I will start to recognise it is already happening. Success is a process and it doesn't happen overnight. Sometimes, when you're in flow that's how the output starts. And it's generated from the input that you put in.

Eventually, you can slow down and take it easy, but I am a firm believer that when you get passionate about something you are all in.

Be honest with yourself

Sometimes we are trying to find the passion that will make us the most money and that is not what this is about. Your passion will make you money if it is your true passion! You can't start something just because people tell you that you're going to make money from it. That's not passion, that's following money and following money will never bring you true happiness.

Back in 2014, I knew I wanted to be a successful entrepreneur and not go back to a job. However, I didn't believe I could be a successful life coach, so I started to follow the money and oh boy... I was attending courses that taught me real estate and how to invest in real estate without having a deposit to invest in real estate.

I started to spread my energy into soooo many things that I was so lost and so tired and exhausted. By the end of the six months, I was seriously questioning if I would ever be successful and make money.

You need to be honest with yourself and dig deep down to understand what it is that drives you. What is something that really makes you feel alive? As a starting point, I suggest you have a brainstorming session and write everything down that pops into your mind.

Lots of books have been written about this topic but, the truth is, passion is not teachable. If passion is an emotion, you can create it for yourself at any time.

Your passion is not outside of you, you can create passion from anything. Sometimes we want a particular thing to be our passion, so we try externally to make it happen. For example, when I saw real estate agents being successful and I wished to be the same, I tried to educate myself and manufacture the passion. At the time, I didn't understand that we create the passion within ourselves, it doesn't just happen to us.

I had the expectation that the passion for real estate would happen to me. And of course, it didn't. If you don't work on it from within, it won't happen!

As you now know, I was basing many of my decisions on fear because I wasn't tuning in to my own values and I didn't have clarity around them. Choose to be honest with who you are, what you want and what type of thoughts you are letting into your mind. Are they positive or negative?

Make decisions consciously of what you value the most. After I realised real estate didn't align with my values, I took some time to think about what my values actually are. I came to realise that mine are love, compassion and sticking to my word. And now I mix all these things into my business. As you make decisions in your business, make sure they align with your values and passion. I now realize I could've brought love, compassion and sticking to my word in real estate, as many passionate real estate agents do.

Always follow your passion

Stick to what you're good at and passion will happen easily and effortlessly. A lot of people try to start a business and they follow what other people have taught and shown them about their passion, or they chase the money. Stick to your strengths, your passion and forget about the money.

Think about your experience and background. When you were little what did you want to do all the time? What was the thing you were always working on? What have you done in the past that you have succeeded in? What problems did you have that you struggled to fix, and then you found the solution? Maybe now, you can help everybody with that same problem by sharing your solution. Create it, practise it and repeat it.

If you believe your passion is going to create products and services that are going to help people, than you will become excited to sell those products to your audience. If you truly believe in your product, you should believe it will change someone's life.

I have found, a lot of business owners forget who they used to be. They forget who they were when they first started their business, and this is something you should never forget.

> 'The biggest risk is not taking any risk... In a world that is changing really quickly, the only strategy that is guaranteed to fail is not taking risks.'
>
> **– Mark Zuckerberg**

The three actions you're going to take from this chapter are:

1. Write down what you love doing, like everything! Keep writing down all the things that you love to do. Write down all the things you are passionate about. Write down all of it.

_____
_____
_____
_____
_____
_____
_____
_____

2. Now put them in order of preference. What makes you giddy? What makes you excited? What makes you feel more alive? What makes you buzz? You can also group them together and sort them into different topics.

_____
_____
_____
_____
_____
_____
_____
_____

Finding Your Purpose and Passion

3. Imagine if you were successful doing what you wrote down for number 1. What would it feel like to be super successful? How would it make you feel to be changing the lives of others? What would that look like? Write it all down. Dream big and dream now!

_____
_____
_____
_____
_____
_____
_____
_____

CHAPTER 3

FAILING YOUR WAY TO SUCCESS

'When you take risks, you learn that there will be times when you succeed and there will be times when you fail, and both are equally important.'

— Ellen DeGeneres

In the first two chapters, you've learned a little about me – and maybe you have also heard some of my story in my previous books, *Follow Me: Shuttt upp and build your network* and *Bums on Seats*. In case you haven't, just briefly, I want to share with you how I went from feeling like a failure to completely transforming my mindset, growing my business and rediscovering who I really am.

As I talked about in Chapter 1, when I was little, my fear of failing meant that I became the best excuse maker. I didn't want to fail, so I created excuses for why I couldn't participate in activities, sports or anything at all. As an adult, after going through countless self-development courses, and becoming a qualified life coach, I came to realise that deep down I was actually terrified of succeeding and making others feel like losers. I was terrified of standing out and then falling big time.

I wasn't sure if it was worth it, to go through all that pain of learning something and then fail. It wasn't worth my time! It wasn't worth the pain or embarrassment I would feel being in front of everybody. So, the easy way out was to just fail. I wanted to be completely invisible. I didn't want to stand out. The thing is, a lot of people who are afraid of falling, are also afraid of success. One of the things I would like you to start thinking about is, what is success to you? What does it mean when you're successful? What does your life look like when you're successful? What happens in your business? When you're successful who are you going to become? I didn't realise how important these things were, in terms of allowing me to achieve my overall success.

I wanted to be invisible. I didn't want to stand out. I wanted to really live my life in the easiest, simplest way, because I just didn't want to fail. I now know that I was terrified of what all the people who knew me would think about me. I didn't want to show them that I was a failure. It wasn't even about the strangers, I didn't care about them, I cared about my friends and family. I didn't want them to think I was silly for putting myself out there on social media. I have so many clients now who have the same fears. So, when you are about to do a Facebook Live, when you're about to do anything on social media, or when you are about to do something out of your comfort zone… what is it that is scaring you? Is it the judgement of other people? Or is it the judgement of your friends and family that stops you?

Success was not for me; I just didn't think I was ever going to be successful doing what I love. I didn't think that I had the charisma to do it. I didn't think I had the energy to be successful. I thought I could be the right-hand woman of someone very successful, but just never, ever, ever thought that I was going to be the one on stage! I never thought I would do anything remarkable because I thought I was lazy. I thought I wasn't consistent enough and I never thought I would be able to run a very successful business on the other side of the world by myself.

> 'Successful people do what unsuccessful people are not willing to do. Don't wish it were easier; wish you were better.'
> **– Jim Rohn**

The thing is, there is way more to success than money. I googled the definition of success and it said, 'the accomplishment of an aim or purpose'. Interesting huh?

It's so true! Many of us are terrified to set goals because that could mean NOT succeeding which equals failure! And let's be honest, nobody likes failing.

A lot of clients ask what success means to me, and honestly success for me is a calling. Success for me is something greater than me. It's something that I cannot stop because the universe is making me do this.

Success is a legacy, a legacy that is going to go through and impact parts of the world. If everybody takes responsibility in this lifetime and starts to create a small ripple effect on their friends and their community, then the world will be a better place.

Accept that success is a process

We all know success is not going to happen overnight, right? It's going to take quite a while to become successful and accept success. Every step of the way, the biggest thing I've done to contribute to my success is to work on my mindset. I believe this is the huge contributing factor that has taken me from zero to a million-dollar business. I've been working on the truth around what I am feeling to understand my true thoughts attached to success and failure. For example, how I feel being on stage, how affected I am when I receive a complaint or get trolled on social media.

> 'A man who has not found something he is willing to die for, he is not fit to live.'
> **– Martin Luther King Jr.**

You don't have to be willing to die for success, but you do have to love someone or something more than yourself. Success is learning how to love something more than yourself. Success is giving and showing up for people. It is making other people our first priority and not ourselves. I used to be very self-centred and it was all about me. But success is not about me. Success is about everyone else. Success is about that passion, that mission. Success is about who else we are going to help and impact. Who's lives are we going to change? Success is that next level of consciousness, and not about you.

This is the biggest thing I've learned in the past five years. I used to think that success was for me, for my ego! Success to me was to look good for my family. It was proving to my school teacher that she was wrong (the one who told me at 13 years old that I wasn't good at English grammar and I should not go to language school to continue to study foreign languages). Success used to be an ego thing, and until that mindset had shifted I was never really successful.

So, my question to you is, what is success to you? And what is failure to you? I don't want you to just write down things, I want you to right down feelings. How do you feel when you're successful? How do you feel when you fail? What are you afraid of? What are your fears when you're successful? What are your fears when you're failing?

For me, success is following your mission in life, following the calling that will allow you to contribute. Life is about us all helping one another. Life is about contributing to universal love and happiness. Success to me is that! You can contribute to universal love by loving and caring for others. That's when we expand spiritually. That's when we remember what we are made for! That's when joy and success stay with you instead of running away.

When I first started my journey into business and personal development, I thought successful people were using others and were only attached to money. I thought they were greedy people and I didn't want to look up to them. Something in my mind was telling me, don't be like them because they're cheaters. They don't do the right thing by others, they use others. So, I didn't want to be seen like that at all.

Many of us have preconceived concepts of who successful people are – and my concepts were not serving myself or others well.

I had to let go of these judgements. I started to realise I was judging successful people, and that's why I couldn't become successful myself; because I didn't want to be judged by others. So, the first step for me to be successful was to stop judging successful people and start seeing them as real people. Every successful person is a real person. They have feelings. They have emotions. I needed to be kinder. Just because someone is successful, we can't just assume they're scum or they're horrible people. We need to be kind to one another. As I started to be less judgemental, I learnt how to see the best in everyone and to love everybody. I started to understand that being successful or not, doesn't change who you are. Success only magnifies the type of person you are! Success only makes that part of you bigger. If you're kind you're going to be kinder, if you're not that kind, you're going to be less kind. And so, success does not define who you are.

Beware of the sharks

In business, you will meet some sharks. I like to call them sharks, because I believe that we are in an entrepreneurship, S-H-I-P. So, we are in the ocean on this huge ship, and you just never know what day you will get to wake up to. You can start with a beautiful smooth sunrise and everything is perfect. And all of a sudden, these huge clouds come over you and it's raining and it's pouring and the sea is moving with waves that make you feel like you want to throw up. And then all of a sudden, the waves subside and the waters are calm the sun is out and now everything is dry and you're safe and good. This is entrepreneurship, right? We chose it. We decided to be on the ship and we can't complain now. And then we're looking around and we're quite lonely in the middle of the ocean until you start to see something in the water and you think, oh there's a group of dolphins and you jump in to go play with the dolphins – but then you realise that some of those fins are not dolphins, they are sharks.

And some of those sharks start to give you little bites here and there that start to create scars. The thing is, we all complain about the sharks and we all complain about how much pain they're bringing us and how much time it takes to close the scar and be healed. But we never concentrate on how much of a blessing those sharks are in our lives. If you don't have the negative, the contrast, the problems, you will never be called on to find solutions. I am the best solution-maker because of all the sharks that I've met in my journey. I teach my clients how to avoid mistakes, however, I do encourage them to take risks and to be prepared to make mistakes. It's inevitable. Because if you don't make mistakes, you're not going to be able to build that strong foundation to surf the huge waves that you come across with a million-dollar business.

When you are in a million-dollar business, you are surfing some serious waves. When I'm on them, I wonder how the hell I got this high and how much pain am I going to go through if I fall from this wave now. Because now the waves are huge, but before they were very small. And so, the question is, are you willing to put yourself in those waves early on, to give yourself the skills to go for a ride when they're back, bigger than ever? Knowing there could be sharks underneath, knowing that you might fall, knowing that you're going to get bitten, knowing that you're going to have to go through some tough times? But once you start to ride those waves, that feeling, that emotion, that connection with the ocean, with the universe, that feeling of fulfillment is never, ever going away. It's something you will crave more and more. And so, the lessons that I learned from Mr Shark, helped me grow. I learned valuable lessons that I may not have learned otherwise, like listening to and following my gut feeling. Sometimes the best thing comes from the worst thing.

And so I challenge you guys to start to make a list of all the things that you saw as problems in the past and think about all the sharks that you've met – then write down the lessons that you learned from them.

Blame them for all the good things they've done for you, not just the bad things. What was the outcome that you achieved because of them? Really dig for the good stuff, which can be hard, because we can easily slip into playing the victim and want to tell a story from a victim's point of view.

My perception of this particular shark was just mine – other people will have another perception of him. Maybe in his eyes, maybe in someone else's eyes, maybe when he told this story, he described me as the shark. Maybe I am a shark in his life. And I'm okay with that. Because if there was a lesson for him in this experience, then I'm grateful that I was an experience for him, that I was a lesson for him, and vice versa. By the way, I did send a letter to this man after many years, explaining that I'm more than happy to pay you the money that you think I owe you for the first few months of my business because I am grateful to you – because, if it wasn't for you, I wouldn't be where I am. I haven't heard back from him. I don't even know if he's still at the same address or if he ever got that letter. But the thing is, I had to come clean. I had to talk about it, because I don't know if I behaved the right way at that time because of the limiting beliefs that I had back then. I was so afraid of being used, so afraid of being not good at business. I was overly protective and maybe, I missed a lot of things along the way – but I wouldn't change any of those experiences. If you would like to learn more about Mr.Shark, check out my book, FOLLOW ME! SHUTTUPP and build your network.

Once you've written your list of your experiences with sharks, and you've uncovered the lessons, now ask yourself, why wouldn't you change any of them? And what would happen if you did? A lot of the time, people say, 'Oh, if that didn't happen, I would probably be so far ahead'. But my question is then, 'How do you know?'. For example, if I hadn't listened to the shark I mentioned above, maybe I would have reached a million-dollar business in 12 months instead of three years? I don't know. I will never know, because it didn't happen that way. Maybe, I would have never gotten a million-dollar business? I will never know. But I honestly believe that what should have happened is what happened. The destiny, the perfect scenario is what actually happened. It's easy to fall into the victim mentality thinking, 'Oh, if that didn't happen to me, I'd now be in a better place'. The question is, how do you know? *You don't*. Anything could have happened to throw things off course. Maybe you got sick or had a car accident. You just don't know. And we always assume that the 'what if' scenario is better than what actually happened. But it's not true. Because what is meant to be is what actually was.

Grace and blame

Grace defines who you are – it is the level of consciousness that helps you accept success. As I got my business up and running, there were many times I blamed others for my failures. Blaming others for what was not happening in my business. Blaming team members, coaches, mentors, family and my dad because I hadn't become successful as fast as I was expecting to.

A huge takeaway from Tony Robbins is that if I had to blame my dad for all the bad things that he did to me, I would have to blame him for all the good things that he did to me too. If dad hadn't been tough with me when I was a little girl, I would have never become this strong woman and I wouldn't have this success mindset. Because of my upbringing I learned to never give up. Yes, I missed out on love growing up, yes, I would have like to be hugged more, but I am the woman I am proud to be because of all the things that I thought I missed. I was able to turn that around, when I could have let it destroy me. I could have let it stop me. I could have let it affect me. I could have stayed a victim and blamed him forever, but I realised that without him, I wouldn't be the amazing woman I am today. I had to switch from blaming him to being grateful. I had to learn how to be grateful and graceful to all the people and all the things that had impacted me in my life. That's when true success started to happen.

The thing is, a lot of people started to see me. I think that people started to see me before I saw me. I think people started to understand the energy and the charisma I have before I even saw it myself. I listened carefully to people and I was so shocked and humbled when people were telling me, 'Francesca, you've got this energy about you. Your energy is contagious'. I just didn't know what to do with it.

Failing Your Way to Success

I remember when I was running events back in 2014, and at the end of my little speech, people would come up to me and ask to take photos with me and I would ask myself, why? Why do people want to take photos with me? The thing is, they saw me, they saw my soul before I even realised that it was coming out, before I realised that I was changing from a judgemental girl to a graceful, grateful person. That is where success happens – when you can live 99% of your time in grace, not in blame. When you can live 99% of the time connected to your soul, and not pointing out all the things that are not working. See, all my life I was always living either in the future or in the past. I was never able to live in the present. I moved all around Europe for years, and I was either missing home, or when I was home, I was missing the last city I was living in. When I was home, I was missing my friends back in the city and when I was in the city, I was missing my friends back at home. I was always missing something, until I stopped chasing, I stopped looking back or looking forward and started to just be present. That was one of the biggest things that I've done to grow my business: start being present.

Embracing failure

So, what if I failed? Well, I did actually! I failed big time, because when I started my business, I made so many mistakes. That's why my business is successful now because I'm able to teach people how to avoid those mistakes that I made. Failure is part of the growth; you want to fail so you can grow and learn. It's this contrast and perspective that helps us become even more grateful. Because if things were going well all the time, we'd be bored by now, right? Instead, when things go wrong, we want to go deep! To understand and learn from this failure, so we can grow and get to the next level in our life or business. I have failed so many times in my business. But the thing is, I've learned from every one of those failures. I didn't let failure stop me. I didn't let failure put me down. I didn't let failure be an obstacle to my success, I learned from failure and I wrote down my failures, and I was able to move myself to the next level.

> 'Only those who dare to **fail** greatly can ever achieve greatly.'
>
> **– Robert Kennedy**

So, what if we change the question, 'What if I fail?' to 'What if I succeed?'. This is the question that got me to success. I started to imagine what will happen if I'm successful. What is my life is going to look like? How many lives can I change, how many people I can impact? It's this outlook that will steer you to the path of your mission. When you are successful, you'll align yourself with your purpose and your mission. Nothing will stop you. Once you get that alignment, nothing, *nothing* is going to stop you. When I found the alignment in my business, I just knew that nothing could stop me. I just kept moving forward one step at a time, one day at a time, following my gut feeling, following what I knew I had to do next. I had lots of mentors along the way and I attended lots of courses. Don't get me wrong – I didn't do it all by myself. Nobody can do it all by themselves. You need to surround yourself with people that will give you the guidance towards the next step you need to take. You have to follow your gut feeling when choosing those mentors or choosing the right people to help you. I have invested a lot of money into my brain and will keep investing in it: it's my most precious asset.

To give you a bit of context around my story, I started running events in 2014, on the topic of mindset and personal development. Within three months, my one on one sessions were fully booked. I started to see other marketing coaches, business coaches and other people that had expertise coming to my Meetup asking me how I did it? How did you get bums on seats? How did you get people to come to your event? That was when I knew there was something of value I could teach them. Something unique I could give them, something that would make a bigger impact than just being a life coach. I decided to focus on teaching life coaches how to have an audience, as this would allow them to have a bigger impact. All of a sudden, my business wasn't about me. By helping other coaches, I was creating a ripple effect. I had a coach at the time too, and I fired him after he said to me: 'Francesca, why would you teach people how to put bums on seats? This is your secret, keep it for yourself and you'll be the only one who is successful'.

There was part of my ego that was agreeing with him and wanted to follow his suggestion but that was fear. I knew that successful people are the ones that share and give as much as they can, they don't hold back on information they just keep giving. So, I asked myself, *What's the point of winning by myself? What's the point of putting myself out there and becoming successful and keeping all the secrets to myself?* At that point, I knew that working together with my clients, we could reach more lives and impact more people. Together we're stronger. I fired the coach who gave me this poor advice and started to teach people how to put bums on seats, because it's all about abundance and there is enough for everyone. It wasn't about just me doing alone. It's not about you doing it alone. It's about togetherness, because that will bring you the most joy.

Be grateful for all your failures

I am grateful to every single decision that I've made in my life, because every single decision I've made led me to this point. In the last four years, I have changed the lives of over 10,000 people. I make a difference every day. If I didn't fail, if I didn't fall, if I didn't go through the pain, I would never have been able to succeed. Every piece of the puzzle led me to be the proud woman who I am right now. Every single failure that you go through got you here, right now reading this book. Failures will lead you where you want to go, if you accept your mistakes and learn from them, instead of blaming them. Don't blame your failures, love them. Love your mistakes, love your failure, love everything that happens to you, because *life happens for you, not to you.* That is one of the biggest things I've learned from Tony Robbins and I will never forget it. Life happens for you, not to you. Life happened for you to get closer to your purpose, to your mission. Life happened for us to get aligned and to follow the universe and to know that we are all contributing toward the same thing, which is universal love. We are all part of this. We are all doing this together. Some people put in a lot of effort, some people put in less, but we all here to learn and grow and feel the universal love.

The three actions you're going to take from this chapter are:

1. Write down all the successes that you have experienced so far in your life.

_____
_____
_____
_____
_____
_____

2. Write down all the failures that you have experienced in your life so far.

_____
_____
_____
_____
_____
_____
_____
_____

3. Write down the lessons you uncovered from those failures that has helped you to grow.

_____
_____
_____
_____
_____
_____
_____
_____

CHAPTER 4

INVISIBLE TO INVINCIBLE IN MY LIFE

'With realisation of one's own potential and self-confidence in one's ability, one can build a better world.'

— **Dalai Lama**

When I started my business in 2014 I began as a life coach. I was very excited about mindset and personal development, so naturally I thought, everybody needed to know about this. I had no idea the business would become successful. It was strange, because I kept hoping it would work, but I honestly didn't believe it was possible at first. I didn't believe I was going to be successful in business. And I was also afraid of not being able to maintain the success if I did get it.

It's fascinating how our mind works… I was worrying about how to maintain the success that I didn't even have yet. It's like worrying about not being a good girlfriend before you even have a boyfriend. LOL #fascinatingbrain

So, I started to subconsciously sabotage myself, and in the first six months of my life coaching business I made $120. For real – $120. No extra zeroes at the end.

I nearly refunded the woman that paid me $120 for three sessions because I felt guilty that she was the only client that had paid. Everyone else I was coaching at the time was for free. All my life, up until that point, I was always trying to please everyone. I wanted to be liked so bad and fit in like everyone else. But then I realised that having a successful business wasn't all about being liked. I was staying behind the scenes, helping everybody at the front to succeed, but not me. Deep down, a limiting belief was holding me back: I am not good enough.

My 30,000 followers think that I'm 'crazy', super-outgoing and an extrovert. Some have even commented that when they watch my Facebook Live, they think I'm too much. I have always tried to avoid being told this because I was afraid of standing out. Before I found my passion, I was always very quiet at work and school. Now that my work is my passion, I've changed this around – I'm very outgoing in my business and very quiet in my private time. I love my alone time; I love relaxing and spending the weekend with my baby boy Ollie.

Invisible to Invincible in My Life

Turning point

To go from invisible to invincible in my business, I had to first do it in my life. I had to be happy with my life, which I had never been before. Growing up, I used to cry myself to sleep. I now recognise that playing the victim was my 'home' and I used to feel loved when I was a victim because I would feel sorry for myself. I would make choices to give me proof of how much of a victim I was: living away from my family since the age of 19 was one of those choices. Now I know that I made that choice because my dad used to admire people who were living away from their family, he used to speak highly of them and I wanted him to speak highly of me.

I have since worked so much on my mindset. I can now see why I chose what I chose, and understand this was all happening in my subconscious.

I used to whine and feel sorry for myself. I used to feel lonely and cry every Christmas and feel very nostalgic because I just didn't want to find the solution. I just wanted to be sad. But I knew there was more to life than feeling sorry for myself, so I started to attend personal development courses and my life turned around completely.

I first saw Tony Robbins at his event Unleash the Power Within in 2014. Afterwards, I thought, *Oh my goodness, this man has changed my life in the last four days. I want to meet him I want to collaborate with him.* The thing is, as if Tony Robbins is going to collaborate with me, right? Who was I? It was not possible, it was never going to happen. But I really wanted it, so I figured I had to find a way to get his attention. So, I wrote a letter. As I got closer to stage with my letter, I was shaking because I thought it was the most stupid thing I could ever do in my entire life. Tony Robbins was not going to read it and was definitely not going to personally help me in my business and in my life. But something greater than me told me that I had to do it, which at the time for this incredibly shy girl, wasn't easy.

I had to make a decision. In that moment. I got closer to the stage and the security guards sent me back to my chair saying don't even try. I thought again, yeah, of course why would I even try? He is never going to read it right? But, in that moment, something inside me burst and I thought, *enough is enough!* Enough of letting other people tell me what to do. Enough of letting my negative inner voice tell me what I should or shouldn't do. Enough of worrying that my dad said that I would never be good at anything. Enough, enough, enough. From that moment I decided: I am going to be in control of my life and I'm never, ever going to allow anything or anyone stop me from achieving my dreams. I felt the urge to run towards the stage where Tony Robbins was. He looked down and he took my letter. In that moment, I knew I was going to be successful! I went back home with a new hunger for life and business. I got the courage to take it to the next level. I have never felt this burning passion before in my entire life. And yes, UPW, unleashed the power within, and was truly a life changing event, and every single time I attend this event, my life and business achieve a whole new level. I have been going twice a year, every year, since 2014.

While I was building up the business, some months were tough and cash flow was a challenge. Many people around me, including my family would say to me, 'What are you doing? Just go back to a job. Just give up. You are never going to make it'.

They wanted to protect me, and they couldn't bear to see me in such uncertainty.

My friends would help me rehearse what I was going to discuss on stage and they would always say that it was bad, like really bad. While I am so grateful for their honest feedback, at the time it got to me. It was just so hard to hear the truth. I had to work out ways for me to stay motivated and keep going instead of letting these comments stop me from achieving my dreams.

> *'The difference between success and failure is not giving up.'*
> **– Steven Redhead, *The Solution***

I remember there were times I thought, *Why don't I just go back to a job? What am I doing this for? Why do I need to prove anything? This is so hard and so stressful.*

I was starting to monetise my business but still, the expenses every month were so high and my income was so low that I couldn't actually pay myself for the first full year and a half. I wanted to make a difference so badly, that I just couldn't see myself going back to a standard job. I couldn't see myself giving up on my business. I couldn't see myself stopping anytime soon.

And I didn't.

So, when do we let that voice stop us? And why? Why is that voice stopping us from achieving our dreams? That voice is trying to keep us safe, right? Ninety-nine percent of our population spend most of their time living in fear, in ego. They settle for their lives and I was not going to let that happen to me.

I had to get people's attention and start working my way up from being completely invisible on social media. To really stand out and build a successful empire, I had to be consistent in what I did online and offline. That was the first step to becoming invincible.

What does invisible to invincible mean?

If you are invisible in your personal life, you aren't showing up for your friends and family. If you are invisible in your business, you are not showing up for your clients and online followers consistently.

A lot of people now tell me they don't have time for social media. But they have to realise their clients are going to watch all their videos, they are going to be loving the content on social media. I just launched a new podcast and all my clients are loving it. So, making time for social media means adding even more value to your current clients and being able to help and impact even more people.

The question is, who do you want to be? Let's talk about mindset at every level, from invisible to active to established to empowered to invincible.

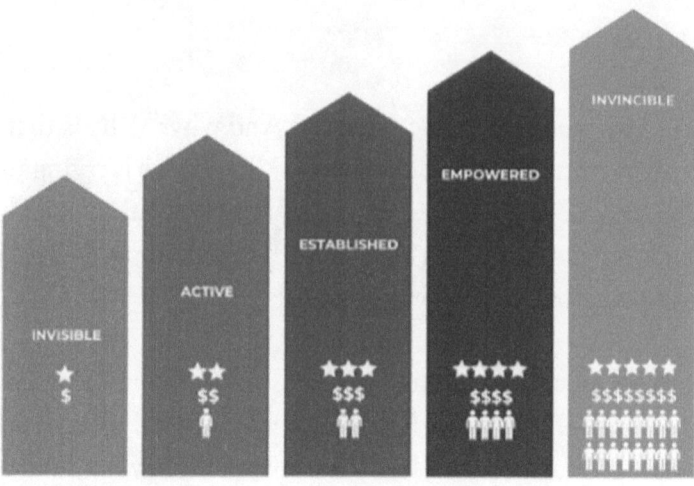

Invisible means you might be afraid of what people think about you. You might have a mask to hide your real feelings. When I was invisible, I wanted to be liked by everybody, so I was loud and out there, but I wasn't being authentic. I wasn't being myself. I was just trying to get people to like and accept me. I was doing things just to get everyone's approval. I was doing what I thought people wanted from me. I was being who I thought people wanted me to be, not who I actually was. I would do things just so people would love me. My actions were all driven by significance.

For you, invisible might mean you are afraid that your friends and family will judge you if you try something new, or afraid you will fail, so you stay safe and stay invisible to avoid that feeling.

Active means that you are not being consistent, or are trying to be someone else just to be liked. Being active in life often means having lots of friends, but not many good ones. You have plenty of connections so that you don't feel alone, but are not really connecting on a deeper level. I have been there. When I lived in Spain, I was the networker of Valencia, everyone knew me, but I had no really good friends. When I moved away, I lost contact with everyone. I was active to avoid hearing my thoughts, I would keep my brain busy with 'friends' so I didn't have to deal with my demons.

Established in life means starting to own who you are, but still being terrified to show your friends and family. For me, the craziest thing about this stage, is that I still didn't even know who I truly was, but I thought I already knew it all. I thought I could do it all on my own. However, that was BS. Nobody can! Nobody can do it all alone, we need friends and family. We need that support network around us who believe in us. I could never have done it without my mum and dad, they were there for me. They were all cheering me on. I started paying attention to those around me, and that is how I found the strength inside me to keep going.

However, many of us make the mistake of waiting for others to believe in us before we go for it and get results. I went out and got results on my own and then they started to support me. I believed in me first and then others started to really believe in me.

Empowered is when I finally started to dig deeper, and I started to understand who I was, and what I stood for. That was when I was ready to stand in the arena. When I was empowered, I was still very much surrounded by fear. By the way, fear will never go away; however, I have learned to snap out of it a lot quicker, usually in a short amount of time. I stay in fear for probably a couple of hours now, when before I used to stay in ego, in fear, for days. So, empowered is when you have more control of your emotions and more control over your fears.

Invincible mindset is what we need to strive for to change the world. An invincible mindset means you make decisions from a place of love not fear. That you are willing to sacrifice for the higher purpose. Invincible means you learned how to love you and nothing can shake you, nothing can stop you. I mean nothing! Invincible is accepting help, asking for help and understanding nobody achieves success alone. We all need others to make a movement, to make a massive impact.

Did I achieve invincible status in my life? Mmmm nah... I do get there at times, but I haven't managed to stay there too long because I always find something else to challenge me so I can keep learning.

Moving beyond fear

Lots of people ask me: what if I can't get over my fears? What will happen to me, my business and my life if I can't get over my fears?

Well if I'd stayed in fear, I don't think I would ever have achieved the business success I have. And I would have never been able to feel the happiness, the love, the fulfilment and the joy that I feel right now in my life and in my business most of the time.

> *'Inaction breeds doubt and fear. Action breeds confidence and courage. If you want to conquer fear, do not sit home and think about it. Go out and get busy.'*
> **– Dale Carnegie**

I moved past fear by surrounding myself with the right people. At every level of the invisible to invincible scale, I've had to let go of people. To keep moving forward, I had to choose to hang out with people that were at my level. When I talk about level, it has nothing to do with bank account or status or anything like that – it's about consciousness. It's about being able to surround yourself with people who are making you a better version of yourself and helping you grow and get to the next level of your life.

What if people don't want to help me? Hmm, that was a big one because I used to believe that people wanted to use me, not help me. As you grow into invincible you will have to surround yourself with people who support you, share the same values and are willing to jump in the arena with you. There will be a lot of people who will point at you and watch you in the arena and judge you and those are the people you want to avoid. The people you want to hang out with and be with are those who are going to be there next to you and trust you, every step of the way.

Success doesn't happen without taking risks, we all know that. If you want to learn how to get on a bicycle you have to get on the bicycle and start riding it so you can eventually stay on it and stop falling. But what are the chances of you falling the first time you get on a bicycle? Quite high! If business wasn't painful, everyone would do it. You have to be okay with it being painful and you have to be okay with failing. Because what are the chances you're not going to make any mistakes and you're going to succeed overnight? It's guaranteed that you're going fail at times, but you have to keep going and you have to keep trying. It's what you learn from your mistakes and your failures that will help you get to the next level in business.

It's the same in business or in life – if you keep doing what you know, you will never grow, you will never explore new things and you will never achieve your wildest dreams. You might be happy with staying in your comfort zone but remember if we don't grow, we die. So, my suggestion if you are afraid of letting go of what you know, write down what would happen if you let it go and what will happen if you don't.

What if your friends don't support you? Welcome to business! Welcome to success. My friends used to message me on Facebook asking me if I was in a cult, which could happen to you too. Your friends, the ones that are not real friends, might leave and they will watch you and judge you and not support you because they're going to be challenged by you. It's not about you, it's about them! They will be challenged about why they're not doing what they should be doing. They are challenged because you're doing it so they might try to stop you so they don't feel challenged, so they don't feel threatened, so they don't feel like they should be doing more too. You might have to let those people go because they have to go through their own journey and you can't let them stop you from achieving all the success you are meant to be achieving. Set them free and always be there for them if they are willing to connect again, but don't wait for them to support you or believe in you. You do it for you, you believe in you first!

It's time to understand where you are at, without judging yourself.

The three actions you're going to take from this chapter are:

1. Where are you at on the scale of invisible to invincible right now? It's okay whatever level you're at, we just need to understand where you are so we can help you go to the next level. Because in the next few chapters we're going to work very closely on helping you go from invisible to invincible, in business and in mindset.

_____
_____
_____
_____
_____
_____
_____
_____

2. Decide where you want to be and why. Not everybody wants to become invincible, some people are happy to get to empowered. What level do you want to achieve and why?

_____
_____
_____
_____
_____
_____
_____

3. Choose a step forward, anything that will get you a little bit closer to the next level – preferably one that will take you to the next level! If you need some inspiration, visit my website and do the invisible to invincible quiz – francescamoi.com/test.

_____
_____
_____
_____
_____
_____
_____
_____

CHAPTER 5

YOUR BUSINESS FROM INVISIBLE TO INVINCIBLE

'Opportunities don't happen, you create them'
— **Chris Grosser**

Now that we have set up the foundation of our successful influencer journey, we are ready to jump into becoming a celebrity online and offline! What do I mean by celebrity? I mean you are an expert and nobody knows about it, right?! Ok, ok, your clients know, but what about the rest of the world? Let's show them you are the go-to expert in your niche!

I built a million-dollar business in three and a half years because I took the steps from invisible to invincible in my mindset and on my social media.

Understanding why I needed to become invincible on Facebook was the key to my success and I know it can be the same for you. So, in this chapter, we are going to work out where you and your business are on the scale from invisible to invincible right now.

First of all, I'm going to be the GPS you need to understand where you're at and discover where you want to be. You know when you are in a car park, your GPS will say find a road that is a straight line, and if you are in the middle of a car park, it's not going to find it? I'm going to step in and be the GPS that is going to help you get out of the car park and find your way to the path that will move your business forward and take it to the next level.

I want to give you some clarity around where you want to be, because a lot of the time in business, we are just all over the place. We don't know where to start from and we often just assume that something is going to take a lot of time, so we procrastinate because we don't see immediate results. But the thing is, in business and especially on social media, you have to be really engaging and be consistent so you can get results. Having clarity on why you need to be active on your social media will help you understand that long-term commitment is the best choice you will ever make and your future self will be truly, truly grateful for it.

First, let's get clarity around your purpose and the structure around your funnel so that you can easily convert your raving fans into clients. This is something that a lot of business owners don't have. They keep following the next shiny object:

> 'Oh yeah, I'm going to create this program and that program...'

They might keep creating stuff, but they never finish it, let alone launch it.

This is especially true of the perfectionists. They never finish anything because nothing is ever perfect enough. The real truth is that they are afraid of failure.

If you launch something that is perfect it means you have launched it **WAY TOO LATE**!!!!

The fascinating thing is that, by trying to achieve perfection, you fail anyway, because not putting anything out there and not launching anything is the ultimate failure. So many times we do this to ourselves because it's the one thing we are most scared of. If you are a perfectionist listen up... STOP IT! It's never going to be perfect. At least if you put it out there, it will get seen and it might change someone's life. It's all about progress, not perfection!

And if you find yourself procrastinating a lot, then keep on reading, because this book is going to help you focus and create a really strong strategy on how to take your business to the next level.

Over the past five years, I have run more than 150 half-day workshops with over 3000 attendees. Of those who attended, I would say 98% of them were invisible, and most of them wanted to stay invisible for fear of judgement. They were terrified to put themselves on social media. They were afraid of what their friends and family would think about them. They were afraid of not being perfect. But the thing is, perfection is never going to get you in the market. So, we need to let go of the fear of being judged. And sometimes that starts from us. We need to stop judging ourselves and we need to stop judging others. When we are afraid of judgement it is most likely because we are the first one pointing the fingers at ourselves and others.

As Brené Brown says:

> 'If you are not in the arena, also getting your ass kicked, I'm not interested in your feedback.'

As business owners, we do care about what other people think and say, and we change and adjust what we're doing depending on what they tell us. It's helpful to hear feedback – however, you want to hear feedback from people who have done it. You want to hear feedback from people that walk the talk. You want to hear feedback from people who know what they're talking about, not people who are just passing their random judgements. Those people do not speak for everybody and not everyone will agree with them. And importantly, they do not have the knowledge or expertise to back up what they've said.

Business is a numbers game. These days, if you are invisible on Facebook and you're not putting some effort into social media, unless you have a huge budget for paid advertising, you're not going to reach enough people. If not many people are following you, there are less opportunities to connect with potential new clients and engage with your existing ones. You're actually doing a disservice to a lot of your clients. So, let's take a look at this graphic again to see how it looks to move from invisible to invincible using social media to grow your following.

Invisible

When you are invisible on social media, it means that your posts aren't working. They get no likes, no comments, no engagement whatsoever. Your motivation disappears and you think, *This is a waste of time! Why am I doing it? My clients are not even on this platform!*

The truth is, the people are there – you just need to find leverage. And the best way to do this is for free, by using the platform to grow your followers organically so that you can get to the next level.

I am going to show you how to do that in this book.

When you're invisible, you feel frustrated, you feel like nothing works. You feel like you are not good at marketing, you feel like you're talking to a wall, so you just give up quite easily. When you're invisible sometimes the only person that likes your post is your mother and that is really embarrassing. So you just want to give up and say, 'Why am I even bothering?' But, if you push through and find the right strategy, you might just move up to active. Worst of all, if you're invisible on social media, nobody's going to show up at your events.

Active

At this level, you are active on social media for chunks of time – this could be a few days, a few weeks or even a month – and then you disappear. You're active for a month and then you disappear for two and that inconsistency creates a meltdown on your number of followers. It is really tough when you are inconsistent to get any momentum whatsoever.

You might also be active in the wrong places. For example, Facebook is a business, so if you are active on the business page, Facebook is saying, if you don't show me the money I will not show you to people. And that is something that a lot of business owners forget. Use the business pages as they are good, but don't solely rely on them – you have to be active in other places too.

Your personal profile is a great example. Be active on your personal profile and be active on Facebook groups, because those are the places that Facebook is actually encouraging and helping you to get as many viewers and as many leads as possible. So being active on social media doesn't mean being active only in the areas where you're going to get business. Being active means consistently adding value and sharing your story, sharing your business and sharing what you are about. If you push through that you will finally get to the established level.

Established

At this point you are getting solid engagement, you get comments, you have likes on your personal profiles and in Facebook groups. Everything you put out there on social media works and you get quite excited about it. But you're not turning those leads into client. You are not actually getting email addresses from them and it's quite frustrating. You might be thinking, *What am I doing this for? Is this ever going to bring me any clients? Maybe it's a waste of time.* At which point, you will likely be tempted to go back to being invisible.

When you are established, you have the momentum, you have engagement and you feel like a powerhouse on social media – *but* you don't know how to turn those followers into clients. You don't know how to make them buy your product or services. At this level, you may be wondering why it's important to talk about personal things and share your story. Always remember that people buy from people, and many will give their business to you because they like you more than the competition. Simply building that relationship with people on social media, allows you grow your network and explode your business, to take it to the next level.

Empowered

This is the point where you start to get enquiries from people saying, *'Hey, I've been watching you, I have been following, you, you are amazing!*

Can you please help me? Can you please tell me more about how can I work with you? I would love for you to be my coach'.

BOOM!!! That's what you want! That's what you want to experience.

At this level, you now know that this social media stuff works. When you are empowered, you feel really powerful – however, there is one downside of this. At this level you're doing it all! You're wearing all the hats, and you're trying to do it all alone. You try to juggle business and marketing and sales and leadership and admin and bookkeeping. And when you try to do everything and you're not in flow, eventually you are going to slowly drift backwards, back into the established, active and, eventually, invisible levels. In the following chapters I will show you how to push through and avoid this, and how to find a solution and get to invincible.

Invincible

Wow!! This is where the magic happens! It's when you have certainty that everything you do in your social media, will sell – you post it, they buy and you can sell whatever you want! Whether it's your products or services, everything you do is bringing you amazing results.

So, do you know which level you are at right now? And have you decided where you want to be? This is super, super, super important.

Understanding the funnel

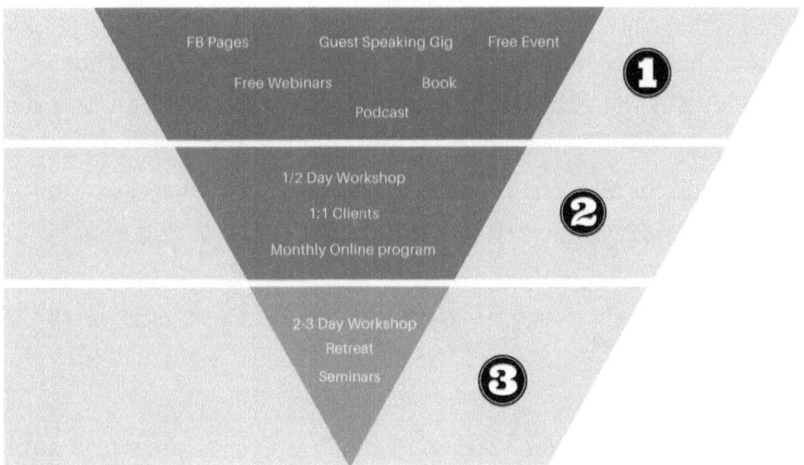

A lot of business owners don't understand the marketing funnel. What has marketing got to do with a funnel? It's a visual tool that is useful, because the shape of the funnel relates to how you convert followers into paying customers. The large, wide top is open and relates to all of the many people you connect with through your marketing and social media activities. However, not everyone you reach is going to become your customer, and that's where the small, narrow bottom comes into it – that is where your niche target market sits, the ones who will become your paying clients.

I call the top of the funnel the Marias. Have you been to Italy? You see the photo here? If so, you must have met the Marias – they are the ones who are always outside the restaurants, but don't often go inside. They don't eat out, they cook for themselves and they love cooking. But the thing is, Franco from the restaurant around the corner knows that the Marias will meet a lot of people and might recommend his restaurant if he is nice to them. So, what does Franco do every time he's got a new dish? He goes outside and asks:

'Hey, Maria, have you tried this? Would you like to try this?'

He gives her a taste and Maria will say, 'Franco, it's amazing. Can I have the recipe?' And Franco will say, 'Absolutely, of course'. He will give them the recipes because he understands the power of giving away free value. Why? Because he knows the next time someone asks Maria, 'Hey, where should I go and eat in town?', the Marias will say Franco's!

Word-of-mouth marketing creates a buzz because people trust their friends. People trust their friend's recommendations and this creates a ripple, as your friends will tell their friends who will tell their friends and it will keep going. This will help build brand loyalty, trust and a buzz.

The question I have for you is: are you nurturing YOUR Marias?

You should make sure that you nurture your Marias, you give to your Marias, you add so much value to the Marias. So, do you nurture your Marias and your Marios? Are you there giving or adding value for free without expecting anything back? The top of the funnel should be the place where you give, give, give, give and give.

In Australia, they call the Marias the freeloaders. We don't mind that these people are at the top of the funnel and are most likely never going buy. We know the more Marias we have, the more followers we have, the more raving fans we have, the more we'll look busy – the more we will look like a person of influence on our social media. This will bring us more clients, which brings us more people!

But this won't happen if you don't give REAL and consistent value.

Everything you do at the top, helps to bring more people through the funnel to the bottom level, which is where you will make your sales. I call the people down here the Sabrinas.

Now the Sabrinas will never interact on your social media, not until they've met you in person and really truly believe they are genuinely going to like you, that you are authentic, that you actually have so much more to give. So the Sabrinas are the ones who are going to watch you and watch you, and watch you, and if they see that you've got enough Marias and Marios at the top of the funnel, then they're going to come into your inbox straightaway to enquire, 'How do I work with you?'. They will be ready, they're not going to fluff around. They have often been watching you for years. But once they're ready, they are ready! They've got a credit card ready, they're ready to buy!

So, the bottom line is, don't waste your efforts marketing to the Sabrinas – market to the Marias, the people who are following you. Give and add value to those people and they will follow in numbers. But remember, your Sabrinas are the right clients. And they will come once you have enough authority and the top of your funnel is full and super engaging.

It seems counter-intuitive, but you need to nurture the wrong people to get to the right people. At first, it's about quantity, not quality.

Now you need to decide: how many people do you want to help?

When I say help, I mean how many people do you want to come through to your highest program? We can only truly help someone when they join our end program, because the more time they spend with us, the more help they will get.

If you've put a small number down then maybe you are limiting yourself? Sometimes business owners put a really high price tag on their services because they 'value themselves'. But the thing is, putting a high price means you are actually limiting yourself, because you can't help that many people. There was one client of mine, who was offering a course that cost over $300 for a four-hour workshop. The price severely limited the numbers as it was really only people who were directly referred that attended. Those people already had trust, so they didn't care how much it cost and just went ahead and did it. But it excluded a lot of others who may have been willing if the price wasn't so high.

Now ask yourself: are you limiting your numbers because you want to charge too much?

Are you limiting your numbers because the middle of the funnel is way too high, and that means your numbers are small? So, if you have four people at the middle level of your funnel, how many people are going to go through to the next?

Usually, out of 10 people, one person will say yes, and there are nine who will say no. If you want to have four new clients you're never going to get there if you charge too high in the middle of the funnel.

A few years back, I realised my prices were too high. I was being selfish and making it all about me. If you think you may be doing the same I have some clear advice: stop being selfish, and start giving!

To get your numbers up, bring your prices down. Start to add value to as many people as possible and understand and see the bigger purpose, the bigger vision. How can you reach them? How can you reach all of your audience? Well, by expanding your following. Over the next few chapters, I will give you a step-by-step strategy to get from invisible to invincible. You're not going to suddenly become invincible overnight, but we're going to get you there if you follow the strategy in order. There will be things that will be time consuming, yes. However, once you do them and you move up the ladder, you won't need to do these little tasks anymore. Now I've got a team that does it for me. But to get here I had to do things that I didn't like to do at times. *Are you willing to do the work?*

The bigger the better

You can impact and help so many more people. Stop thinking small and start thinking big. If you're thinking, *Oh, I'm just happy with five clients*, why? Why are you thinking that you can't help more than five? That is not true! I used to think that. I used to think that if I just keep my workshop at 10 people, I would be able to add more value because they would spend more time with me… that is total BS.

The more people in the room, the more valuable it becomes, because when you have a lot of people in the room, they will network with each other. There is going to be so much brainstorming, so many more brains together which is powerful, which is energy, which is vibration.

Don't limit your numbers because you're afraid of not adding value. That is your self-doubt and lack of self-worth coming through. So, don't let that stop you. I did it myself for many years, and actually, I still do it. Once I got to 20, I wanted to stop at 21. Then I went to 30 and I wanted to stop there and so on. Just keep going. Because the more people you have working with you the more people you can reach and the more people you can impact. Start accepting and allowing people in!

I find it fascinating how many people deliberately choose not to use their personal profile on Facebook because they want to keep their personal life separate from their business. Every single successful person I know has maxed out their Facebook friends, which is 5000. You can't have more than 5000 friends on Facebook. And there is a reason why: because Facebook knows how powerful that is. Facebook knows that if you have an unlimited number of Facebook friends, your business will explode and you won't need to pay for Facebook advertising until you are ready for the million-dollar business. People want to be closer to you and you need to allow them to be close to you, so they can follow you, so they can start to trust you even more.

Using your Facebook personal profile will allow you to make a greater impact and help more people, because they're going to see the real you, not the fake you. And if you are concerned about what your friends and family are going to think, ask yourself, are you really going to let a small number of people limit your mindset and stop you from achieving your dreams? Don't play small!

There was a lawyer who was allowing people to friend him on Facebook. When I met him, I asked him, why, and he said, 'Francesca, if I didn't do that, I wouldn't get any clients'. He said he is active on his personal profile, and is active on Facebook groups that will give him referrals – and the referrals will give him momentum to get more and more and more clients. And because he's the only lawyer that allows people to friend him, he said it's perfect!

> 'Your competitors will do it if you don't, so hurry up, don't play small. Don't be too special about it and let people in!'
>
> **– Francesca Moi**

A lot of people ask me, 'What happens if you stay in a word-of-mouth business?'

Well, when you're in a word-of mouth-business, if you don't add new leads into your funnel, the funnel will die. Anything that doesn't grow will die. So, imagine that the only people who come through to your word-of-mouth business are referrals. To get to that point, at some stage you must have been networking to get your business out there, doing everything in your power to get clients. Eventually you start to get clients referring you to others, so now you don't have to do the two things that most business owners hate: marketing and sales.

And so, people are coming to you and are already sold and want to work with you. Everything is going fantastic, so you stop doing marketing and sales, and just wait for people to send you new clients, which is a great thing, apparently. But what eventually happens if you don't keep hustling, don't keep bringing NEW people in, is you're going lose it all. People are going to stop referring you and, eventually, you're going to stop putting yourself out there at all. So it will start to slow down. And when you try to go into marketing and sales now, it's different. Ten years later, you don't know what to do or how to put yourself out there. What you used to do at the beginning, doesn't work anymore! So, it is really dangerous to have a purely word-of-mouth business and only rely on that because it is not sustainable. Obviously, it's a great place to start and if you feel like business is good, then great! However, you don't want to stop there. Keep doing what you're doing, but also look for ways to bring new leads into the funnel.

Have you ever asked yourself…

What if you sabotage your self-growth?

As I shared earlier, you may subconsciously sabotage your own results and need to start over. You can avoid self-sabotaging to a certain degree if you can learn to recognise the symptoms, but eventually you will sabotage yourself in some way. When this happens, it is important to notice and learn. Sabotage is a normal, common pattern. Remember, your business is a 3D printout of your thoughts, so working on your mindset is so important. If you don't work on your mindset, you will eventually start to struggle with getting more clients and growing your business. Self-sabotage happens when thoughts creep in like, *I'm not good enough. I don't deserve this success!* Any thoughts along these lines will create a lot of self-doubt, which then turns to sabotage. So, work on your mindset and you'll avoid sabotage big time!

What if I'm not ready?

Guess what? You will never be ready. People are waiting forever to get a dog or have a kid. And guess what, there's never a right time, there's never the perfect time. People sometimes wait to live with someone, to break up with someone because it's never the perfect time! There is a holiday coming or there are parents coming and visiting, there is a party for someone that we know and so we keep pushing things back that we know we should be doing because we don't think we're ready. It's not the right time, right? But the thing is, we're never going to be ready so you might as well start now.

What if I have multiple products or businesses?

Oh, dear I get this a lot! Focus on one. Focus on one, stop trying to do it all! The jack of all trades never gets anywhere, get to know the one product, one service, choose one of those and make a six-figure business from that. Once you get to a six-figure business, you can start adding more to the top of your funnel, but don't create another funnel. Keep adding to the same funnel over time. The funnel is one, the target market is one, the niche is one and you just keep adding more products into your funnel and adding more value to your funnel but you're not changing. If it doesn't fit in your funnel, don't do it! Learn to say no so that you can concentrate on what you know works.

The three actions you're going to take from this chapter are:

1. Draw your funnel in three simple levels.

2. Put the price you are charging at each level.

_____
_____
_____
_____
_____
_____
_____
_____
_____
_____

3. Explain your funnel to someone in less than a minute.

_____
_____
_____
_____
_____
_____
_____
_____
_____
_____

CHAPTER 6

INVISIBLE TO ACTIVE

'People don't know what they want until you show it to them.'

— Steve Jobs

Now this is the time where we start to get shit done. I am going to show you literally how to go from invisible to invincible step-by-step in each chapter from now on.

Have you ever done one of those DISC profiles or wealth dynamic profiles? Well if you haven't, I strongly recommend you do one as they are the best way to discover what type of personality you have and what comes natural to you.

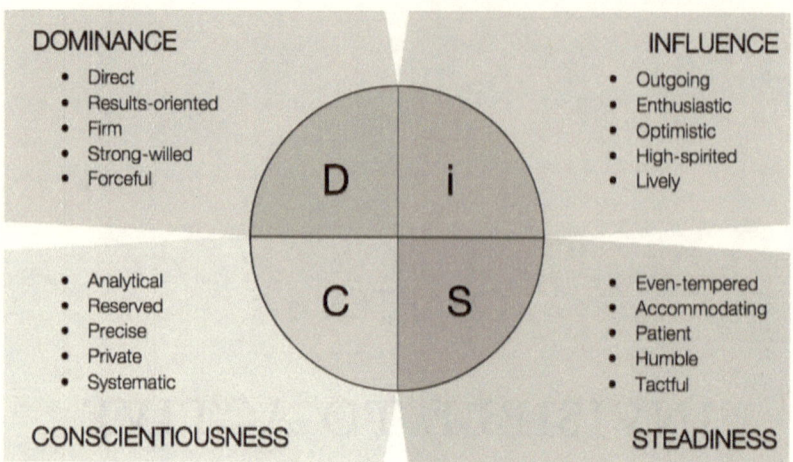

I'm an action taker and I wasn't always like that. I used to be an excuse maker. As you know, I was the number one excuse maker, but now I love to take action. I love to get results fast and do so as much as I can. I hate those workshops or books that all you do is read about other people's success and then you go, *Ok that's great but I have no idea where to start from or how to do this.* I'm not like that! I'm going to get you to take action. So, get ready to put your book down when I say so and take some action and then come back and keep reading.

So here is the HOW! Firstly, we'll look at how to get from invisible to active.

If we stay invisible, we can't help people. Staying invisible on social media means that nobody is going to see you. If you are going to stay invisible, you're not going to impact your potential clients or even people that will never pay you. You can make a difference to them if you stop being invisible. One time, I was a guest speaker at an event and a lady approached me after my talk to say:

'Francesca thank you so much for your talk, it's been inspiring and all. But I don't know where to start. I'm terrified of putting myself out there on social media. I don't want to do this Facebook Live. People will think it's all about me, I'm not one of those people that want to make it all about me.'

I get this a lot and I get it, so I said, 'Well, you don't have to make it all about you. In fact, it's not about you! It's about looking at what people need and wanting to provide that on social media. Everything you're going to be doing to stop being invisible is for them, not for you. If you want to make an impact and make a difference you have to show up. And if you want to make an impact you have to be a leader, and the first step is to influence yourself. The more ownership you take of your own life, the more you're able to build that authority in others' lives. You need to be the first person you influence, so you can create positive change in the world'.

If we don't take steps out of our comfort zone, we won't be able to build trust. And if you don't build enough trust with your potential clients, they're never going to sign up to your programs or services. They're never going to be working with you. They're never going to see you. They're going to see your competitor, not you. So, stop being invisible because it is the most important step in growing your business – you need to start building momentum and be seen.

If you are still afraid of judgement, it's because you're still focusing on you instead of on them – it's not about you. When you focus on yourself, that's when you think, *Oh, are people going to judge me?? Are people not going to like me??*

When you focus on others, it doesn't really matter who you are. I've learned by spending a lot of time on stage that if I'm on stage and I'm in my head, I don't connect with anybody. But if I'm on stage, and I actually concentrate on the people, then magic happens because they feel me, they feel the energy, they feel my intention, they feel that I'm there to support and help them and I'm not there to make me look good. It's not about me, it's all about the audience.

Stepping up in the Facebook influencer journey will allow you to give and to contribute. As business owners, influencers and leaders we have a duty to show up and contribute and be a giver by adding value. If you are invisible, you're not going to be able to do that, which means you're not going to be able to contribute, which means the universe is not going to give anything back to you.

It's time to be a leader, to speak up and spread your message. If you don't do that, your competitor will. Take ownership of the outcomes of your decisions, even if it's a mistake, be open to admit your mistakes and tweak your decisions along the way. You are an expert in your niche, and you could be the biggest kept secret. It's totally up to you – are you going to be an expert nobody knows about and only help the people in your small network or are you going to be an expert and be well known? Do you want to be the person everyone knows so that you are the go-to expert, therefore getting more clients and making a greater impact? If you stay invisible, you are selfish. Think about how many people would appreciate your help. And if they could find you easily it would be even better. If they can't find your social media, you're not going to be able to help them. So, stop being selfish. Don't make it about you, even if you don't want your friends and family to see you. You are a vessel of this amazing purpose and if you don't show up, if you don't know how to spread your word, you're going to die with your voice inside. Is that what you want?

What does invisible mean?

Invisible means that you have no following, that you have nobody liking your posts, that every time you are on Facebook or any social media it gets frustrating and feels like a waste of time. Invisible is that you rarely hear the bling of your social media app on your phone. Nobody's actually tagging you and the notifications are not coming. Or, maybe they are coming but it's never about you or your posts. Your timeline is all about others, and you are sharing other people's posts instead of creating your own. I find it fascinating when people share other people's posts on their own timeline. It appears that you have no value to add and that's why you share other people's posts. But I don't believe that! I know everybody's got value to add, YOU have value, YOU have a voice, YOU have a message. Stop keeping it to yourself and start helping other people who need to hear you.

My team and I do a lot of research on social media and when someone is invisible there is not much posting on their personal profiles. All we see is other people's posts and not much posting from them. Don't let this be you.

When I was invisible, I was using Facebook to keep in touch with my family and friends from Europe. And I was terrified of using it for my business. When I started to post a little bit about me and my new journey and I started talking more about my passion, most people were supportive of me. And it just became so exciting to share my passion with others.

There was one person that had a negative comment, a dear friend of mine from Europe asked me if I was okay, if I had started a cult in Australia? He said he was genuinely worried about me, LOL.

I wanted to give up, I wanted to stop using my personal profile, but I didn't! I didn't let someone else's limiting belief stop me from following my dreams.

If I let that one person stop me, I wouldn't have had the privilege of speaking in front of thousands of people at my workshops, events, on stages and online and I wouldn't have made the impact that I've made over the last few years. I could never have grown a million-dollar business on the other side of the world all on my own!

Are you going to allow people to stop you from achieving your dreams? Are you going to allow small-minded people to stop you from making the impact that you know you can make?

If the answer is HELL NO, then start friending people on Facebook. Yes, on your personal profile! Start a genuine conversation with them. Add value wherever you can. Don't sell! Social media is not for you to sell, but is there for you to give.

On your personal profile, you really have lots of support. You have friends and family, you've got people that you've met, you've got people that have interacted with you. Most likely, most people will be super supportive. A lot of my clients are terrified of putting themselves on social media, on their personal profile. And when they start doing it, they find it very surprising how many amazing friends they have, how many people are willing to support them and follow their journey. There are people that have been following me for the last six years and they message me all the time saying, 'Wow Francesca I have been watching you since the beginning, you've been doing amazing! Congratulations!'. So, if I didn't share my story, my journey, when I did I wouldn't have inspired other people to do the same. And now they are able to connect with me and actually see the real me.

Remember, one of the values we stand for is that people are opportunities. There are 2.2 billion people actively using their personal profile and Facebook groups. You should leverage from those instead of trying to use Facebook business pages, which is the slowest way to use Facebook. I mean, you still want to use your business page but remember that all these people you have as friends, they really are opportunities. They are people, who know who they know, and who knows what they're going to bring into your life, into your business. So, stop hiding and start sharing with them what you're doing, and what are you about. Talk about your story, your day.

Some people ask me, 'What do you mean share a story of my day? I do nothing all day, it would be a very boring story!'. My answer to that is, 'Well get a life! Make your life more exciting! Go and do stuff, go work from a café instead of working from home. Go and catch up with clients, connect with clients, connect with people. Do things that will trigger you to share about your day and create your own stories'.

That way, you can start posting things like, *I just met with that person today and we talked about that blah blah…*

You can you also share what's happening in your life with your daughter, with your son, with your husband, with your co-workers, with anybody around you. There are lots of things that you can talk about and share on social media that will benefit the whole world. So, start sharing!!!

A lot of the time when people are invisible it's because they've tried in the past to grow a following and they haven't succeeded. They tried a couple of posts. They shared personal things on social media and felt frustrated and disheartened that nothing happened. Nothing happened, there was no momentum, so they gave up! They gave up way too easy. But think about it – if you are planting seeds in a garden and you're watering them for three days only, can you expect the seed to grow just in three days? No, right? Seeds need time! You need to keep giving, keep showing up! Keep being consistent and that will create momentum. For people to relate to you, you've got to be seen and being invisible is not going to allow you to do that. So, don't give up! If you're not getting any likes or any comments, it's because you've been under a rock for the last five years. So, stop it! Get out from under your rock and start posting, start engaging, start commenting on other people's posts so people see you. You've got to start slow, but remember this is a long-term vision. If you stay invisible, in a years' time, you're not going to have any clients or be making an impact. Everybody started somewhere – so why not start today?

Is it ok to talk business to friends?

A lot of people come to me and they ask, 'What if my friends get annoyed with my posts about my business? Isn't Facebook for, you know, personal and social?'. Okay, so your friends are going to get annoyed about you posting about your business only if they are not very good friends. They're not going to be supporting you, in your mission, I mean. Sometimes we surround ourselves with friends who are going to make us smaller, they're going to make us feel like they want us to be smaller so they don't feel that bad about themselves. The thing is, you need to start to surround yourself with people that are 'higher' than you and who are better than you in areas you want to improve. It helps if they're hungry to grow with you, and can push you to achieve more. You can't worry about annoying people who want to stop you from being successful. That is a limiting belief they can worry about, while you focus on your raving fans and what they need. And I know by now you'll be like, I don't have any raving fans, what are you talking about? Yes, that's because you've been invisible! So, you're going to stop being invisible and start to put yourself out there so you can build raving fans, so you can get people to see you, and want to hear more from you. You want to get to that point! One of our clients was invisible and all of a sudden she started to post and post consistently and she started to get clients saying, 'I need to hear that!' and 'Thank you so much for posting that, I really needed some inspiration today'. There will always be people who need to hear from you. So, stop being invisible. Stop worrying about what your friends and family think and maybe start to choose who you hang out with.

People need to model someone, they need direction, they need community – and every community needs a leader. You can be a leader in your own way. I try and use compassion as I lead because I recognise everyone is on a different journey and if you can relate to another person by putting yourself in their shoes, you can understand their struggles and pains. And you can help them learn and grow. Clients will run away if they think you can't solve their problems.

The other question I get a lot is, 'What if I want to use my business page only and I don't want to use my personal profile on Facebook?'. Well, why would you do it the hard way? It's not working! The business page doesn't work, unless you pay for advertising. As I said earlier, the business page is for business which means Facebook wants your money. So, a business page is not going to get any interaction until you start to use your personal profile. Once your personal profile is big enough then people will go and stalk you through your business page in other places. So, don't limit yourself by thinking that because you're a business, you have to use a business page. Just be open-minded and use what is going to work in your business to get you and your business out there.

But what if it doesn't work for me?

Well, that's impossible. The strategy works for everybody, every business, every product or service that you provide, because people buy from people. People want to get to know you before they make an investment with you. Whether it's a $5 investment or a $10,000 investment, it doesn't matter. People need to see you, trust you, like you, before they even consider doing business with you. So, stop trying to hide behind the name or brand or your business page, get out from under your rock and start to show people the real you. Take your mask off and choose to be authentic. Authenticity is the key. You want to let people see the real you, not the business side of you.

The three actions you're going to take from this chapter are:

1. Double your Facebook friends in the next three months.

_____
_____
_____
_____
_____

2. Join three Facebook groups where your target market is and add value.

3. Post once a day on your personal profile on Facebook.

CHAPTER 7

ACTIVE TO ESTABLISHED

'Discomfort is the currency to success.'
– Brooke Castillo

Does it feel like you're not going anywhere? I get it. When you are invisible, it can be very frustrating. But we're going to get you out of that level once you have built enough trust. You have to trust the system and then your clients will trust you! My clients follow these strategies and they all tell me when they get to the end of this level, they start to hear from their followers:

> *'You are everywhere. Wow, your business is exploding.'*

This is a great sign!

When you hear people telling you on Facebook or Instagram that you look very busy and everything is active, it's a fantastic place to be. Keep going, because that's when you're going to start converting leads into clients. Don't give up now, you've come so far! In this chapter, you're going to learn how to move from active to established. It's not going to happen just by reading though, you have to take action!!! You must implement the strategies to get yourself there. Have you done the homework from the last chapter? I am watching you!!!

> *If you haven't, stop now and get it done. It's not going to work if you don't work for it!*

Have you taken the Invisible to Invincible Test yet (francescamoi.com/test)? Even if your test came back as active, still go back and implement steps in the previous chapter, as all these levels offer priceless opportunities to grow your social media following.

At the active level, people will start seeing you as the go-to expert in your niche. This means you are giving and adding so much value that people begin to recognise you have something special to offer. They'll see that you have an amazing gift and you are ready to shine. People will start to follow you and see the value that you have. But don't expect to get these results from your business page organically – remember, to use your personal profile and grow that first. The more people you have on your personal profile, the more people are going to go through your business page. Don't expect results overnight. Remember this is a long-term strategy that is going to work if you work it!

The active stage is about testing, measuring and doing more research to understand who your target market is. You need to learn what your audience needs and understand if you are in the right community.

By the way, if you're still not convinced about the Facebook personal profile, I get it, you don't have to believe me… but go in and see it for yourself. Go to your Facebook home page and start scrolling. You will see four posts from your friends, in groups or in their profiles, the fifth post will be a sponsored ad from a business page, then more posts from friends. You never, ever see a post from a business page on your home page unless it is a sponsored ad.

See? I told you! Now that you have seen it with your own eyes do you believe me?

It's all about trust

At this point, start to concentrate on building trust. Here are three tips I share with my clients to grow their following and build trust:

1. Post at least one post on your personal profile once a day
2. Post in a couple of different Facebook groups and start to interact with people on your social media
3. Repurpose your posts on your business page.

Honestly, I don't spend much time on Facebook. I just check it in between meetings or when I have a free moment. I check my notifications to see if there's a comment for me or if I have been mentioned somewhere. By constantly checking notifications and responding to every post, it continuously builds trust on your personal profile and then people will start to stalk your business page too.

For now, focus on getting clients one on one. Forget about one to many – we need to get you fully booked one on one, even for just a month, to be able to move to one to many.

Your ultimate goal is to expand and be able to go one to many eventually, because that's how you're going to be able to impact more people and make a difference in many, many, many people's lives.

A lot of business owners concentrate on the breadcrumbs. What I mean by that is they spend so much time and energy to try to sell programs that are $20 here, $5 there or maybe try to meet clients before the one on one sessions. And that is all breadcrumbs!

What you want to do instead, is create something long term, create something big, a program that will truly transform your clients. And then you will be able to make a difference in their lives.

If you're working with clients in a one-off session, you're not going to be able to make a lasting impact on their life. You need to really think what is best for your clients – what do they need, what is the program or platform or package that they need to really experience a lasting change. Don't waste time on the breadcrumbs.

You need to give them more by adding more value. You want to add more sessions into a package, or to offer three courses for the price of two. You want to add more value and make sure people have multiple points of contact with you and not just a one off. Remember, the top of the funnel is all about quantity and is all about building trust.

The more people you have at the top of the funnel, the more people are going to go through your funnel organically and you won't have to forcefully push them through it.

While in the active level on social media, you'll find the business page is still getting little to no interaction. Obviously, this is quite frustrating. So, what I want you to do is shift the focus and instead be active on your personal profile.

Most active people have a word-of-mouth business and think people aren't following them. But you don't know that, you haven't seen them. Remember the Sabrinas, the people in the bottom of your funnel, who are not interacting at the top of your funnel? They're going to watch you and stalk you, and they're going to just check you out for a while in silence, until you have wowed them. Once you wow them, they're going to come and be ready to work with you. So, at the active level, you generally don't get many leads from Facebook or Instagram. You just get people to watch you and stalk you. Usually the clients who resist the most in using their personal profile are the clients that succeed the most.

Do your research

Ask questions on Facebook groups to your target market about a pain they have. This has been one of the biggest strategies for me to get myself out there on social media and really build the trust in Facebook groups. I was doing research and I was asking questions, and I was getting people to really engage with me. Don't ever assume that you already know your clients or their wants, because you don't. So ask them. I used to go on Facebook groups and really talk about their pain. For example, I would say, 'Hey guys, who here wants to run workshops and what's the biggest challenge you have when running workshops?'.

You can follow a similar formula to find out what you need to know from your followers too. I suggest you talk directly to them. For example, ask them what their biggest challenge is in getting healthy? Or in getting bums on seats? Or in marketing? Or whatever! Use your expertise and ask them. And then, with all those replies, you can do a Facebook Live, you can do another post, you can add free value. Don't send them into your business page. Don't try to sell to them. Just add, add, add as much value as you can. Concentrate on three groups you want to post and interact with daily to build trust. But be in as many groups as possible and try to be active in those as well.

It's time to go live

Finally, once you've done all these things, you'll be able to start doing Facebook Lives. Facebook Lives are amazing, as they give you the opportunity to build trust with people. Your followers will see you and get to know you what you're all about. It gives them an insight into who you genuinely are. They get to know the real you – not the mask, not the fake one, just who you really are.

And here's a tip – rule number one on Facebook Lives is that you never, ever, ever watch it back!

Keep in mind, most people are not going to watch the whole Facebook Live but they're going to watch parts of it and if they like it they're going to start to drop what they're doing to jump on, support you and start becoming a raving fan. They're not going to become a raving fan from one Facebook Live so don't do what most people do. Most people go and do three Facebook Lives and when they get no results and no clients, they think it's a waste of time. No! It's like anything – it takes consistency and work.

If you go to the gym a couple of times would that give you results? No, you need to do it consistently! You need to go four or five times a week to get your muscles defined. If you don't, you're going to struggle to get any results. The same goes for social media. if you do a Facebook Live once a week, you're not going to get anywhere. But if you do it, two or three times a week, you're going to start to see momentum, you're going to start to see people liking what you do. Also, doing a live the same time everyday helps as well because you'll start to get into a routine. You'll find you will be able to give more value because you can start to plan ahead and structure your live.

I get asked a lot, 'What if I don't want to do a Facebook Live? Can I just become the expert in my niche without doing that?'. The truth is, NO. The question you want to ask is, why don't you want to do a Facebook Live? Do you not want to do a Facebook Live because you're afraid of judgement? If that's the case, let's do a game. Let's start with you – stop judging yourself and stop judging others. So, I give you that challenge right here and I hope that you accept it. From now on, every time you find yourself judging yourself or others, I want you to find three positive things about that person or thing you are judging. Deal?

You're missing out on educating your audience if you don't show up on Facebook. You are going to miss out on giving free advice. Remember when I talked to you about Marias and Marios? They are the ones to get a free recipe from the restaurant Franco's – they are the people that get really excited, become raving fans and tell others all about it. They are most likely never going to buy from you but they will follow you. And when you have followers who care about what you do, the Sabrinas, the people at the bottom of your funnel, are going to think that you're famous and successful, and that's what we want.

Consistency is key

Now, what if nobody replies to your questions or comments or engages with your posts? Well, nobody's going to reply if you don't do it consistently. You have to get yourself out there. You need to do it consistently. And eventually you will start to see momentum. When you see one person commenting on any of your posts you have to go and reply. Because imagine if someone meets you, and every time they meet you, you never talk to them, you never reply to the question, you ignore them completely. They're going to stop talking to you. And it's the same with social media. If you don't reply back to every single comment that you get, people are not going to go back and comment again because they're going to feel like it's a waste of time because you don't acknowledge them.

Okay, what if I start to do Facebook Lives and then I'm not consistent, does it mean I'm wasting my time? Well, the key to this organic strategy is to be consistent. Put it into your calendar, do whatever it takes to show up on your social media. It won't work if you're not consistent. And remember, this is not a chore: it should be done with passion! Keep showing up for your future self. Think about it – when you have an appointment in your calendar, you don't forget about it or cancel it. So put a time in your calendar to do a Facebook Live and don't cancel it. I never go away for months at a time, I keep showing up. Stop finding excuses. You should be excited to show up on your social media. You should do everything possible to make sure you go online regularly and share your message.

The three actions you're going to take from this chapter are:

1. Ask a question a week in different places, groups and always reply. Add free value.

_____
_____
_____
_____
_____
_____
_____
_____

2. Do at least one Facebook Live a week. The more you do the better results you get.

_____
_____
_____
_____
_____
_____
_____
_____

3. Work with a coach on your mindset around serving and following.

CHAPTER 8

ESTABLISHED TO EMPOWERED

'Transformation is my favourite game and in my experience, anger and frustration are the result of you not being authentic somewhere in your life or with someone in your life. Being fake about anything creates a block inside of you. Life can't work for you if you don't show up as you.'

– Jason Mraz

How are you going so far? Were you able to do the homework from the previous chapters?

Hold on tight and be patient.

At this level you will feel like you're giving so much and nothing is coming back. You may think, *Hold on a second, all these people are only wanting free stuff from me. I feel like they are only using me. I don't get it, I feel so used and my time is wasted. Social media is not for me; maybe I should do other stuff instead of consistently giving so much value without these people noticing it.*

The established level is where you feel good for a bit and then you start to get a bit annoyed and frustrated with your Marias. This is where you start to get resentful. *Hold on, I give you all this stuff and you never want to be my client? Ahhhhh!!!* The first thing that I would advise you to do is to concentrate on being grateful.

Be grateful for new Marias!

I honestly would not be where I am now if I didn't have my freeloaders. All those Marias never pay me a cent, but they are always there in every webinar, they do participate in everything I offer, either free or at a very low cost. I feel grateful because they are making me look successful on social media and they promote me without knowing it. A simple thank you post from these people is a milestone for me. The more mentions I get, the more people will get to see who I am and what I do. They create an illusion of having so many followers and because of that, people will start to check me out and stalk me. Isn't that amazing? Remember, these Marias are bringing you more clients in the long run. So be thankful to them and be grateful.

This might be the hardest step of the process because you're doing a lot of free stuff. And you probably still won't see the money coming in, despite all your hard work. You may forget why you're doing this and want to give up. But please hold it together. And remember I'm going to show you, in this level, how to start to monetise and, how to get to empowered. This is where we start to get some clients. Consistency is key.

The goal is to start monetising your Facebook, Instagram and any other social media platforms you use. I know if we don't start seeing money soon, you will want to give up and we don't want that!

I don't want you to get frustrated at these platforms. I don't want to see resentment from you. We don't want to see any of that.

We want to keep you at the highest energy, the highest level. And we want to keep you consistent. Always remember that people need your help!

People need to see you and I promise you that this will turn into money, there is no way that it's not going to work.

You want to invest time in building a strong following, because this is something that will work for you long term. What we've been doing is building your raving fans, which is so important because they will be the ones to continuously watch you online for years. I get messages every day from people who say, 'I used to watch you five years ago when you first started, you're amazing'.

You can start your own community at this level, because now you have a following. Now you start to have raving fans. Now you have the momentum. It's time for you to start that community of Marias — the people at the top of your funnel who will most likely never buy anything. Many of my Marias are in my Workshop Secrets for Coaches and Expert Facebook group and Meetup group. The meetup group has over 5000 people now and the Facebook group is over 10000. The Marias are adding to my social proof.

We want to build this tribe so that you can step up as a leader and so you can use this tribe and this community to lead you to massive success. It's really the place where you're able to position yourself as a leader, and tell people that you have a community, you have people that are listening to you so that you can interview them. You can collaborate with successful people because of this community. Don't ever take your community for granted and don't ever give up on them because they are going to be your leverage to start monetising your following.

Leadership puts you on a pedestal and helps you influence and impact more individuals. This component of leadership is sharing the journey and helping others recreate that journey. Once you have a strong community, you can now start to move from one on one to one to many and get more clients from either of these two.

So how can you leverage from your presence? Start by elevating your energy and creating engagement in your community. If you are still following your passion, you don't need to find external energy, it should be within you and this is what will be pushing and motivating you to keep showing up. When you are creating engagement, participate with a passion and wholeheartedly. Do this by sharing and leading with love, and when someone interacts with you, respond to them every single time. It's not about you, it's about how we show up more powerfully for the next person.

Remember, if you're at this level, we're going to start to look at outsourcing and delegating. If you don't do that, you're going to get stuck. Too many business owners fail in business because they don't delegate. They try to do it themselves, they become control freaks, they become perfectionists.

When I was at this level, I started to feel that I was professional and I started to get some clients from my networking, and from other places. So, I needed to make sure that I looked professional on social media. I started to put my mask back on. I started to be fake again. I started to be more professional and people started to not resonate with me, so I was actually losing a lot of my followers.

This is where you need to choose authenticity. You need to choose to be authentic every day. You need to choose to be vulnerable. You need to choose to keep showing up and keep giving and adding value.

If you stick to this, you're going to go to the next level, which is empowered. Which is so exciting because that's when you finally start to get more enquiries, start to get people reaching out and saying, 'Hey, I want to work with you'. Remember the Sabrinas who are going to be watching you and wanting to work with you? Now they're just about to ask you to be their coach or be their mentor. So just hold tight and stay there.

Empowered is where we're going to get you a virtual assistant so you can get more engagement while you're delivering to your clients. So, don't give up now. You've done most of the hard work. Once you've achieved what you need in the established level, we're going to get you to empowered. This is where magic happens!!

So how are we going to get you there?

First and foremost, we're going to start your own Facebook group and Meetup group. Now I do teach this as part of the Academy Family Academy. I spend quite a lot of time talking about it to my clients, about a couple of hours on just teaching how to do it specifically for success. Anybody can start a Facebook group or Meetup group. But guess what? There are so many out there. There are so many Facebook groups and Meetup group. Why yours? Why would yours be different? Why will people join it? Why will people be wanting to participate in it? What's in it for them?

You want to start your Facebook group and Meetup group only if you have followed the strategies and you are actually at the established to empowered level. You don't want to start a Facebook group or Meetup group when you're invisible, because the only person that is going to join will be your mum. And we don't want you to only hang out with your mum. We want you to hang out with your Marias, with your followers, with the people that love you and engage with you.

You want to focus on getting emails and making sure you don't put all your eggs in one basket. Don't leave all your followers on Facebook or Meetup. You want to start to get emails. Start running webinars, weekly webinars where you add massive value with the PowerPoint presentation and other free content that you can offer so people start to give you their email addresses and you start to take advantage of your Facebook group and Meetup groups. You want to grow this group organically. Don't ask people if they want to join, don't just be a spammer because nobody wants to join a group like that. And make it about them. What's in it for them? Why would you suggest to someone to join that group? What would be the benefit to them to join that group? You want to create a group where people are really going to feel supported, feel connected, feel they've got a chance to promote their business, feel like there is something in it for them. The community needs to be based around them, not you. The community is going to be based around building trust and adding value. You want to have amazing speakers come speak at your events because the more value you add, the more people will attend.

This is where you can also start to run live events like meetups, networking events, meditation classes, anything that you want. Start by running them in your Meetup group. This will bring you closer to your audience because you can get to know them. You have to spend a lot of time promoting and engaging in this group because this is how you will start to get clients. If you don't get engagement, this group is not going to get anywhere. The main focus, especially on the Facebook group, is to get this group as engaged as you can. Ask them questions, ask them what they need, get them to reply, get them to promote their business, get that engagement going, and it will be the difference you need in your business.

Many people ask me, 'What if nobody joined the group? What if nobody shows up to an event?' Well, it means you haven't given enough value to people. It means you haven't done enough, it means that you haven't promoted it enough, you haven't put enough passion into it. You haven't shown them the value in attending the event.

We went to one of our Academy Family member's events in Cairns not long ago, and it was amazing. The energy in the room, the passion that she had on stage, the community that she was building, the guidelines that she had about building that strong community of helping one another, not selling to one another. That's what you want. You want to create a community of people that feel like you are going to give them value like they've never seen before. You want to wow them, and you want to keep them engaged and keep them there.

What if you don't know how to promote an event?

Well, this is where I'm known to be the Meetup Queen! I know how to promote events and how to get people to show up to them. I co-authored a book called *Bums on Seats* and I've written another book, *Follow Me: Shuttt upp and build your network*. If you want to learn how to get people to show up to your events, check out those two books and they will give you all your answers. And if not, just reach out to me or my team and we can help you by signing you up to one of my seminars.

What if I want to just be online? Do I have to run events? Well, I believe that a combination of online and offline is the strongest strategy ever. Because when people see you having real people in your rooms, they're going to start to assume that you have value. Don't get me wrong, my friend Amanda, has been doing everything online and she's got a really successful business. However, since she's stopped doing the offline stuff, she sees the difference in how much more connection and how much more of a higher level program you can offer because you get to build that extra trust and rapport with people.

The three actions you're going to take from this chapter are:

1. Keep doing the things you did to get to this level and don't give up on those strategies. It's time to bring it all together and make it happen.

_____
_____
_____
_____
_____
_____
_____
_____

2. Start your Facebook group, open your Meetup group and start collecting emails.

_____
_____
_____
_____
_____
_____
_____
_____

3. Look into hiring a virtual assistant who might be able to help you in the business, so that you can concentrate on growing the business, not being in it.

_____
_____
_____
_____
_____
_____
_____
_____
_____

PS if you are considering joining the Academy Family Academy, wait, and let us show you, step-by-step, how to start a Facebook group, Meetup group and we will find a virtual assistant for you.

CHAPTER 9

EMPOWERED TO INVINCIBLE

'The biggest adventure you can ever take is to live the life of your dreams.'

– Oprah Winfrey

This is the part that is going to be fun. This is the part where you start to get clients, start getting enquiries and start to make a real difference in people's lives. You should start investing in team members to help you out with managing all your social media platforms. However, there is a certain way you should do this. I made a big mistake a few years back which I'll share with you now, because I really don't want you to make it too.

In 2016, I was building this massive business and I was so active on social media. I was literally everywhere. Then I started to delegate to my virtual assistants and they were doing the right things and everything was working well. And then what happened? I started to get stuck leading the team, teaching things to the team and I started to forget to show up online and offline. I stopped creating content on my social media platforms. I didn't do any Facebook Lives. I didn't show up and this caused my followers to stop following me. This is why you need to learn how to find the balance between delegating but also showing up because in 2017 disaster struck. My followers didn't connect with me anymore, because it wasn't me anymore. It was my team. I don't want this to scare you and I don't want this to stop you from having people on your team. You need to monitor and manage your team, but you also need to make sure that you show up on your social media. They can spread the message for you, they can help you with being everywhere. But you need to keep showing up and to not forget about that.

So, it's time to scale your business. That means you're going to be able to help more people. and you're going to be able to engage with more people. Having a virtual assistant doesn't mean being fake. There is a right way to do it and a wrong way to do it. I will show you in this chapter how to hire a virtual assistant to manage certain aspects of your social media, without losing your followers like I did.

A virtual assistant will help you gain momentum to start leveraging from all your hard work. They're going to help you be able to do what you're most passionate about, which probably is teaching, coaching and spending time with your clients. A VA can keep the momentum going on your social media while you do what you love.

Before you become invincible, it is important that you have that certainty and backup. At invincible level, your business is going to explode, and you know that anything you put into social media will be successful – events, webinars, anything you do is going to be successful.

You're going to be able to have fun because you start to monetise your leads, so you don't feel like it's a waste of time. You can finally make the most of your following. But remember, this is where it's tempting to start hiding and put on a mask. Don't do it!

Be you! It is so important!

Here's what I really want to share with you. A lot of people at this level start to fake it, they start to put the team forward, they start to hide behind the computer and not show up on social media. Remember to find your balance.

Invincible is a feeling, not a step. It is the most exciting level, because it is the place where you get to celebrate your wins. But remember it's about the journey and you should celebrate it the whole way through not just at this point. I know sometimes when you're not making any money it's hard to find reason to celebrate, but remember you need to be grateful, to be happy for every single Maria that follows you. You need to be happy for every like, for every comment and for every reaction. If it wasn't for those people, you would not be at this level. You should be proud of what you've created and how many lives you have already impacted, and are still impacting. There is also pain at this level though, because like in every level and stage of life, we have the good and the bad. And this time it is the growth pain! You will get to this point and you will have to take a step back to go forward in your cash flow, in your time. Also, you have to learn to delegate. I felt like I became a manager, not a business owner and I hated it. I hated coming to the office, because I was stuck dealing with problems. All I was doing was coming to the office and putting out fires here and there and dealing with problems with clients. It's all I was doing and I used to hate it. So, I learnt how to delegate so that I didn't have to deal with all the problems myself all the time. I taught my team how to find solutions and encouraged them to come to me with solutions to solve the problems – and it made a massive difference!

So that's one of the first things we're going to have to teach you is how to delegate.

My first virtual assistant had very little experience. I really, truly believe that it's best to find a virtual assistant that is not overly experienced rather than hiring one based on their experience alone. Look for a virtual assistant who is very smart and has a university degree or other qualification, but who has not worked in a virtual assistant position before. That way, they are keen to learn and they're hungry to succeed because they want to work from home. It's likely they want to be at home because they have family commitments, so they are going to be really keen to work from home and will be loyal to you if you are a good boss.

How to be a great boss

Being a good boss doesn't mean you let everybody do whatever they want whenever they want. You need to keep them accountable and make sure that they're doing their job. At the same time, you need to make sure that they love what they do.

I bet if you have ever tried to find a personal assistant, you went onto a virtual assistant hire website and did an interview with them. And when I do interviews, I usually look for their personality. The personality is the most important part because you can't teach that. So the first thing I'm looking for is, I don't want anyone with a victim mindset working for us. I don't want anybody that is going to be stuck in a negative mindset so that you have to praise them all the time, because there's no time to do that in the business. At the same time, you want someone who is willing to learn and willing to grow with the business. And if they do that, they're definitely going to get praised and definitely going to get reward for their efforts. So you want to give them some scenarios like, 'Okay, if this problem happened, how would you solve it? What would you do? How would you deal with it?'. I want to see how honest they are.

I have also found that employees from some cultures are used to fixing their own problems and rather than telling you there's a problem, they try to fix it themselves. And while initiative is great, this can sometimes be a disaster. For example, when I started working with my first virtual assistant, she was amazing but was also making mistakes. It's important to be patient with your people because sometimes as business owners, we assume that someone knows how to do everything. At first, the way that I would delegate was like, 'All right this needs to be done go and figure it out'. And that was it. And this poor virtual assistant of mine didn't know what to do or how to do it. And so, she tried to figure it out on her own because she knew how busy I was. So, when I said, 'Look, this needs to be done and we need to send an SMS to all the people that are coming to the workshop next week' but I didn't show her how, she went into TextMagic, which is the platform we use to send bulk messages to people. And she accidentally added every single person that attended the workshop in the past and sent the message to them all. Now, that was 50 cents per person which at that time, for me, was a lot of money. There was 350 people in my database at that time who had come to my workshop, so that mistake cost me over $175. At the time, that was my rent, and I didn't have much cash flow as you can imagine and was really struggling. And my first thought was, you are fired! But at the same time I started questioning myself – how many times have I made a mistake or stuffed up? Plenty.

When mistakes are made, it can be tough and at that time I didn't want to keep her working for me anymore. However, I couldn't have been more wrong because it turned out to be a blessing and she is the best virtual assistant that I could ever dream of. It was me who needed to learn – how to be patient, how to spend time with her and show her things properly and understand and accept that people make mistakes. So, although I wanted to fire her, I didn't. Instead, I sat down with her and I told her how to do it next time and how to do it properly. But, before I learned that lesson, I sucked it up and I got really upset with her. And then she tried to fix the problem by sending another message to every single person, 350 people, to say sorry. That was another $175! At that point I wanted to go and take a flight to the Philippines. Obviously, I didn't do that. Then I sat down with her again and explained that from now on, every single mistake that you make big, small, whatever it is, just feel free to come to me, talk to me and together we'll find a solution. That way, we can grow and learn from one another. We can create systems from it. We can create procedures to help any future employees to not make the same mistake. I also promised her that I would never get upset or grumpy if she came to me with her mistakes. I would just be here to support and help her so that together we can create an empire. And guess what? We did create an empire! Sometimes we talk about how we used to spend hours on Zoom talking about how this is going to become a big business. And look at us now – 13 people working in the business, everything booming, everything growing. It's just a blessing to have her on the team and have her with us and I'm so grateful that I didn't give up on her and she didn't give up on us. So, it's been a team effort and together we surely have grown an empire.

Now another growth pain is cash flow. Cash flow will probably slow down at some point, it just happens to every single business. At times you'll feel like, 'Right now I'm empowered, I'm nearly invincible and I still have problems with cash flow, what the hell is going on?'. It's normal. It is a growth pain that happens to every single businesses out there, so all you need to do is to watch your cash flow and make sure that everything you invest in is something that is going to give you a return on investment. Invest in mentors and strategy, in courses, in anything that's going to help you grow, your mindset grow and therefore your business grow.

You will need to start to get some systems in place, you need to start to be organised, you need to start to use Asana, you need to start to use Slack, you need to start to use Ontraport. They are amazing. They're insane! And it's what you need in your business. It took me years to find the right system to use. I am providing you with a PDF (francescamoi.com/systems) for you to download to get the info on all the system we are using so you can find the right ones for you.

Finding the right VA

Now what we get asked a lot is, 'What if I can't find a good virtual assistant?'. Well, at the Academy Family Academy, that's what we do! I realised how much time and effort it takes to find a loyal and outstanding virtual assistant, so now my team and I find and train VAs for all our clients in the VIP program. Once again, my tip is to find someone who is not experienced in the virtual assistant world because if they are, that means they are working already for multiple companies and they're never going to be committed and loyal to you.

Have you ever asked yourself…

What if I don't have cash flow to move forward?

Well, welcome to business! You have to go back to basics, go back to doing what you need to do to get more one on one clients. Go back to making those 10–20 phone calls a week to get clients on board. Don't ever give up! We all have problems with cash flow, we all have ups and downs. Just put yourself out there. Have faith that being invincible is actually happening and you're committed to embrace it. Believe that you can do it. Believe this is what your future self will want. If you don't believe in yourself, who will? You need to believe your products and services are making a difference and that they are good enough. You have a purpose to give your life meaning, and once you truly believe this, you will continue to stand up to the occasion and become someone who is going to provide change in this world.

What if I'm not even close to being invincible yet?

Well, maybe you are expecting that invincible means you have everything perfect, guess what? It's never going to happen. We never have perfection in business. We're always going to have growth pains, we are always going to have the good and the bad side. But guess what? Go back to the invisible to invincible test we did earlier in the book and see where are you at and if you're not at the level where you should be, then go back and read through the steps I gave you in the last few chapters and make them happen. Remember, consistency is key!

The three actions you're going to take from this chapter are:

1. Spend some time working on your funnel to reassess it and make sure you're focusing on just one funnel, and you're not following the next shiny object.

_____
_____
_____
_____
_____
_____
_____

2. Hire your first employee in your office. (I gave this challenge to one of my clients the other day and now everything is exploding for her).

_____
_____
_____
_____
_____
_____
_____

3. Have a virtual assistant working with you if you are at this level. When I was at this level, I had three VAs – so if you haven't done that yet, make sure that you hurry up and get yourself a virtual assistant!

CHAPTER 10

STAY INVINCIBLE

'Business is a spiritual journey.'

– Tony Robbins

While it is hard work getting to this point, staying invincible is where the true challenge really lies.

When I got to invincible, I fell into the ego trap. I started to work really hard on my personal profile and everything started to gain momentum. So, I felt like I was famous. And when I got famous, it was just so hard because now I didn't have time to talk to my clients or to my followers. I started to get team members to talk for me and that upset a lot of people. It upset a lot of my followers. Some people thought I was making a fool of myself, but I literally had to delegate and start to move away from doing some things and try to get my team to respond to emails and messages and things like that. So that was initially very hard. And then I started to believe I was too cool for school and I was too good for doing things myself and I started to become out of touch with my followers. I started to forget about them. I started to not be active anymore. I started to train and monitor the team and I fell out of my flow. I lost my flow.

Marketing is my expertise, business knowledge is my expertise but anything that requires admin skills, I'm not that good at. I started to feel very out of flow and that affected my social media following, because everything started to slow down and I went back to established and then back to active and then, eventually, back to invisible. I had to work really, really, hard to get the business out there. I also had Facebook advertising going, so I was paying a company $2,000 a month to run Facebook ads for me and it was about $5,000 a month in Facebook advertising. And at the end of 2017, all my Facebook advertising was not working anymore. I discovered that what some companie do is to pay people to get bums on seats for them on Facebook ads, and from each ad they pay about $100 to $300 per person to show up at their events. So that's quite a lot of money. But it was working as a strategy. So, I started to put more and more of my budget into Facebook ads every single month until the beginning of 2018. Suddenly, it was costing $400–$600, and one person cost $1,500 to get their bum on a seat.

It's crazy how much companies spend in Facebook advertising if they know how easy it is to put bums on seats without spending a cent. All you need to do is follow the strategies in this book and BOOM you will get bums on seats. This was a result of me thinking I was too famous and not making time for my followers. In the next chapter I will talk about ego and how to stay centered and not let your ego control you.

Now that was devastating. I started to think, *What am I doing? How am I going to stop this?* In three months, I had spent $40,000 in Facebook advertising. In the next chapter I will talk about ego and how to stay centred and not let your ego control you.

Never lose sight of what's important

I had to realise that it was super important to be consistent and stay on top of my following and keep giving to the Marias. I had to learn how to nurture my own following again, how to show up, how to be consistent. Facebook shouldn't be a chore. It should be a pleasure, it should be something that you're excited about, to show up on your social media and post content. It should be something that you just can't wait to do.

You want to be in front of your followers consistently. When you're ready to pay for advertising you will get massive results. You want to keep posting, you want to keep showing up, you need to keep being there for them so that you can make the most out of your Facebook advertising.

People that see your Facebook ads will then start to follow you, they will start to see your personal profile. They will watch your Facebook Lives, they will read your posts, they will start to make their mind up about who you are and if they want to work with you. And if you don't have a following, if you haven't got momentum on your social media, then they're not going to be convinced.

You need to continue building trust and ticking boxes, which I will talk more about later. But it is all about making sure people are continually seeing you, that you're building trust, that they're liking you, seeing the accountability, the credibility and the social proof. Everything you're doing is actually helping them get closer and closer and closer to becoming your clients.

If you stay invisible you will never be able to do that. Being invincible means you're going to start to get interviews, you're going to start to get media and you're going to start to get recognised in your niche and beyond.

Don't risk losing everything you have created. If you stay invincible, you're going to be able to maintain, grow and scale it. Don't go back to being invisible.

The shocking truth of this chapter is that it's all too easy to fall back to invisible even if you are invincible. Because invincible is not a status you are awarded for life, it's a journey. And you want to stay there as long as possible. However, sometimes ego or not being organised is going to send you all the way back.

The journey

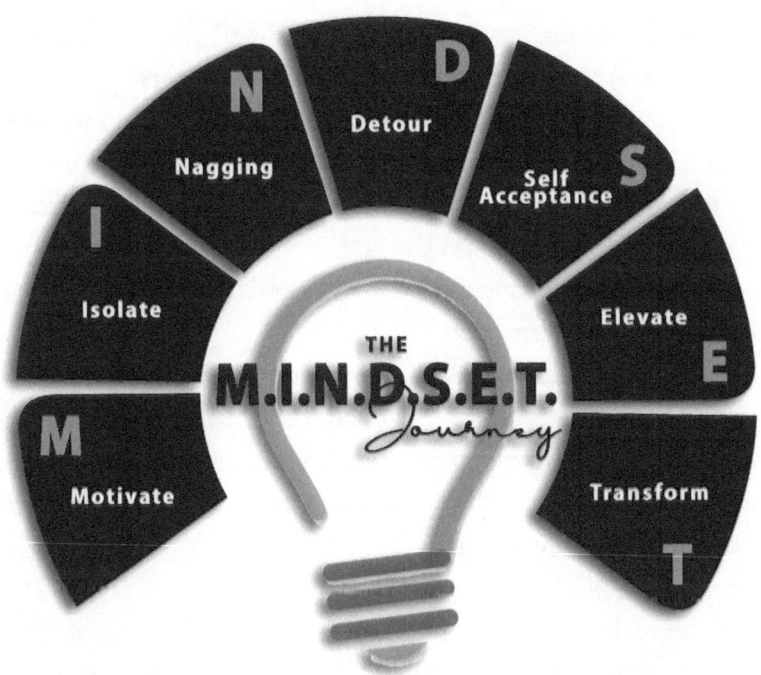

Whether in our personal life or our business, we all go through a personal development journey. I want to walk you through the different stages of this journey, so you can pinpoint where you are at and how you can continue with your journey if you're stuck.

It all starts with motivation. You feel **M**otivated and start believing that this personal development stuff is amazing, and you spend hours researching and learning everything you can about it. This causes you to **I**solate yourself, because you're spending so much time researching and learning, you begin to think you're smarter than everyone else. Your ego takes over and you don't see other people and other people don't want to see you. Then you think you know it all. So, you start **N**agging everyone around you about everything you have learnt. You then try to teach others, but they don't want to listen to you because you have isolated yourself for so long and are now trying to teach and sell them things they do not want. After you're done nagging, the universe gives you a **D**etour because you aren't doing what you're supposed to be doing. You should've been helping people. At this stage, you've probably forgotten your passion and who you truly are. So, now you have to overcome the detour. You go through a period of **S**elf-acceptance, self-growth and self-love. You discover and accept others as well and you elevate to the next level of your growth. You are now able to **E**levate others without judging them – you are no longer nagging them. You truly want to help them. After this step, this is when you **T**ransform and you feel invincible. You are the most powerful you have ever been and you become so motivated that you start the journey again.

To stay invincible, we have to get over ourselves and think about the bigger picture and continue adding value on Facebook Lives and Facebook posts. Now it's time to leverage from the followers, to get emails and get clients.

In this invincible stage you're going to start to do your Facebook Lives weekly. You're going to start to run webinars, you're going to start to add value consistently so that you build a bit of a routine for people to know that at that time of the day you're going to be there for them. Let's choose a time. Let's choose the time for you to do a live. For me, it's my weekly trainins in my Workshop Secrets for Coaches and Experts Facebook group. Every week for half an hour I share tips and things that I've done in the business to grow from zero to $1 million business in just five years. How did I do it? What happened? What steps did I take exactly? Every single week I spend half an hour for free, adding massive value. These webinars allow me to get emails and get in front of people every single week. I build trust and tick those boxes by sharing personal content.

The value in these regular Facebook Lives doesn't stop there. My virtual assistants transcribe the Facebook Lives and turn them into content so that we can post every single day in multiple places, pages and groups. This creates momentum and is a great way to repurpose valuable content. Now, all I have to do is post every day on my personal profile. I don't have to worry about any of the other places because the team are taking care of the repurposing and posting. But, if you're not doing any Facebook Lives, you've got nothing to repurpose. So, make sure you do your work so the team can do the rest.

Now it's time for you to leverage on the social proof. It's time for you to show photos of you online, offline, wherever you are, to showcase the success you've been having. This is not about bragging and being like, 'Y'all, look at me, look at me!'. It's more about showing proof that you are making an impact and reinforcing that you can help them. If people don't know you, they're not going to trust you. They need to see that you have achieved success with other people, that you are the expert, that you have the experience. Then they can trust you and go, *All right, I need to go to this person.* I mean that's what you want, you want them to think, *That's it, I'm in!*

I get lots of people that come to us and say, 'Oh Francesca I've been following you for years and I've been watching your journey. I've seen so many lovely stories of your clients who are doing well and I need to be with you'. Now some people watch it and think, *Oh my goodness, all these people are doing so well but they're not like me,* and they need to tick more boxes for them to actually decide they are in. Every person is different and some people need you to tick more boxes than others.

Have you ever asked yourself…

What if I want to delegate all this social media stuff to my team and I don't want to do any social media?

Well, you can't really do that. That is the lazy way to do business and as a business owner, people need to know who you are, people need to know where you are at. Once you get to invincible you might say, 'I now don't have to do as much, I can show up at the office at 10:30am, I can show up only for the events. I don't promote the events anymore. I just have to do maybe every now and again a couple of videos here and there'. Maybe eventually you can do this, but once you get to invincible you need to do your work. You need to put yourself out there, you need to show up. You need to do everything you can for people to get to know you and that includes Facebook Lives. If you don't do Facebook Lives, people are not going to really know who you are!

What if I don't want to keep being active on Facebook?

Well, you are making it about you. You're thinking about how much time it is going take you to be active on Facebook, when all you should be concentrating on is how many lives you're going to change when you show up on social media. How many lives are you going to change by adding value? You don't want to make it about you! You want to make it about them!

What if I want to stop Meetups and Facebook and live events and I just want to do everything online?

Well, a combination of offline and online strategies is the most powerful strategy, don't give up now! We still run our own offline strategies, we still run events offline, and that gives people the extra trust. Once you've done it for a few years, you can eventually stop and do everything online if you want to. However, the way to make an impact, the way to change people's lives and to really turn them around is to make that message strong enough to bring them into a workshop, bring them into an experience of two, three, four days of seminar or retreat, so you can actually teach them *and* show them how to get into the new routine.

The three actions you're going to take from this chapter are:

1. Do a Facebook Live weekly and repurpose it into a webinar.

_____
_____
_____
_____
_____
_____
_____
_____

2. Get your virtual assistant to transcribe it.

_____
_____
_____
_____
_____
_____
_____
_____

3. Repurpose it into multiple contents for social media.

_____
_____
_____
_____
_____
_____
_____
_____

PS: If you are looking for a virtual assistant, that's what we do as a business – we find and train virtual assistant for our clients (our Academy members). If you are interested in the Academy Family just send us an email at info@empoweringevents.com.au and we can give you more info about how you can get a virtual assistant who can share your workload so you can be even more focused on the business!

CHAPTER 11

STAY CENTRED AND GET RID OF EGO

'Your ego is your soul's worst enemy.'

– Rusty Eric

This is my favourite chapter because it's all about staying out of ego, which is not easy. As you move through each of the levels, you will often find yourself stuck in ego. Sometimes there is ego about the fear of not being good enough or not being able to maintain your level of success. Other times, it may be because of a fear of success, or fear of being a failure. When you're invincible the biggest fear is now that you start to get recognised. You start to get recognised at events, at pubs, even at dog parks. True story. People started recognising me in multiple places where I never thought anybody knew of me, both in my own city, and interstate.

It is surreal when people stop you in the street and say, 'I've been watching your videos, thank you so much, you've made a really big difference to my life' and you just think, *Wow, like really? Oh my god, stop it.*

Eventually my head got big, and at times I thought I was famous. And now that I was successful, people needed to make an appointment to talk to me.

After a while of thinking this, I could see it was getting in the way of making friends, because I was afraid that people wanted to use me. That people didn't see the value in being a friend without having to use me. I'm not sure that I managed to stop that ego from happening completely, but I am working on it.

When I had my first $220,000 month I started to think, *Holy shit, I must be good at what I do.* Lol. But does it mean anything? Making $220,000 or making $20,000, does it change anything?

Does it change who you are? People say that money changes you. Tony Robbins says that money expands who people really are. So, if you are a greedy person and you get money you become greedier. If you are a happy person when you get money, you get happier. If you're depressed person when you got money you get more depressed.

Money doesn't change who you are, it just expands your personality.

Don't allow that limiting belief to stop you. If people recognise you or not, it doesn't matter because you are still the same person. I remind myself every day that I would be no-one without my Marias, without my followers. I can't give enough thanks to all the people who have been there and supported me throughout the last five years in this amazing journey. Literally, I do meditation and thank them, because without them I wouldn't be here.

So are you nurturing your clients enough? Are you giving enough? Are you warming the people that are in your tribe? Or are you just thinking what's in it for you?

People love genuine leaders. I was reading a beautiful book by Brené Brown *called The Gifts of Imperfection*, and in it she says, *'Authenticity is not something that happens to you, it is not a personality trait, it's a choice! Everybody's got a chance to be authentic it's just a choice. You choose to be authentic or you choose to be fake, and being real is harder than being fake. You don't want to fake it till you make it.'*

You want to be real. You want to take the mask off, even if it is hard, even if at times you want to hide, even if at times you don't really want to show up that way. But you have to because people will see it.

Personal growth is the business growth. In business, so many times, we are looking for answers, we're looking for a solution. But the thing is, the problem is, as business owners, we have to keep growing. As we keep growing, we need to learn, we need to get to the same level. We need to make change, we need to embrace change, and a lot of us are scared of that.

But why is it important to change?

This is mind-blowing, because if you want to grow your business, you have to let go of what you know, and change. Once you learn to be okay with change, you can grow. And this was one of the toughest things that I have ever done because when I got the million-dollar business, I thought I knew everything I needed to know about business. I had all the answers and I didn't need to learn anything else, right? Just super wrong. I didn't want to let go of what I knew. But in order to grow the business and take it to the next level, or even to maintain it as a million-dollar business, I had to change. I had to change how I was working as a leader, I had to change how I was working as a business owner, I had to change how I was working as a CEO, and I had to change how I was dealing with clients. Even though it was scary, even though it hurt, with every ounce of my body, I had to do it. I just know there's something on the other side that is going to take me to a whole new level. And so, I learned how to embrace it. It doesn't mean that I'm not afraid of it. Change is the beginning of the next level of your success. So, if you don't embrace change, you're never going to grow, you're never going to take the business to the next level, you're never going to be able to be a better version of yourself. What if change is the catalyst of your growth? If I didn't make changes in my life, I would definitely not be here right now. If I didn't make changes in my relationships, I wouldn't be where I am now. If I didn't let go of people that were holding me back, I wouldn't be where I am now. This year, I'm going for a $3 million business. Would I be able to create a $3 million business if I didn't let go of change? If I didn't let go of old procedures, if I didn't let go of old staff members, if I didn't let go of my old office, if I didn't let go of my old business coach and hire a new business coach, would I be where I am?

If you want to grow your business, you can't make the decision with the same identity. Five years ago, my decisions were based on a lot of scarcity. Now, my decisions are mostly driven by abundance. I'm making the decision now with the mind of a $3 million business thinking, all right, if I'm going to continue to grow my $3 million business, how do I need to make decisions now? If I keep thinking and making decisions with the mind of a million-dollar business, I'm never going to get there. So, I need to change the way I make decisions. I need to change the way I think about my business. I need to change the way I think about my employees and my clients. Oh boy, I had to change the way I thought about my clients every step of the way.

Growth is also very much about your mindset. In my company we call it the Academy Family mindset, because as you know, business success is all about mindset. Without it, you're not going to do anything. It's also a key reason why you are invisible or active or established, and not yet at the invincible level yet. Because of what your brain is telling you is possible and not possible. Every individual is free to do whatever they want. I'm not going to tell you how to behave, that's up to you to decide. I do believe that you can't make new decisions with the same identity. For example, my decisions used to be based off of scarcity, so scarcity came my way – and when I started to base my decisions from being invincible, I became invincible. It was the limiting beliefs that were holding me back for so long,

I'm not saying it's easy to change; there are fears attached to it. I have changed my mind about many things in business. I am willing to grow and take it to the next level because I am not attached to anything that I've created. You just need to remember that everything happens for a reason and when you create change, that's when the magic happens.

Nowadays, there are too many businesses that just care about their business and their numbers, not realising how their mind reflects the outcome of their business. And that's one of the reasons why I created the Academy Family Academy. I wanted to have a supportive community of like-minded individuals that truly help each other to take their business, their life and their influence to the next level. For me, that is the most important thing in business.

I always tell my clients that if they want to be part of a community, they need to work at it. They need to make the effort to get to know people, go to other people's events, give support, and be the first person that reaches out. The bigger the community, the more we all win. The more we get to support one another and the more business we're going to get from one another, right? Because in business and in life, everything happens for us. Everything happens for a reason. Every little obstacle that happens to you happens for you. And when I truly understood that, everything changed in my life: my business, mindset, money, cash flow, bank account and friendships.

I started to see everything as a blessing and everything as a learning opportunity. For every experience, I tried to uncover what we're going to learn out of this. The game changed. And I would love you to see that as a blessing for yourself. Remember that everything you see in others that you don't like, is a mirror of yourself. And this is something that was really challenging for me when I first heard it. I was like, 'I don't like people who judge'. Well, guess what? It's because I didn't want to admit that I was a judgemental woman. I now see people that judge in a different light, because I know how hard it is to stop judging, because I've tried for so many years now. When I see people judge, I can feel compassion for them. I don't judge them, because I used to do it too.

If I die tomorrow, I have no regrets. No regrets because I did everything I could to make a difference in this world. If I die tomorrow, I know that I did everything in my power to share my voice, to share my message. Have you? Could you have done more? Can you do more? Well guess what, the good news is you still have time. Don't waste it. Don't waste the time that you have right now. Put yourself out there and promote your business, your message and your voice as much as you can, as loud as you can, without changing who you are. Just take one step at a time, one day at a time, and everything will work itself out. Do the right thing and you'll see everything will align.

The resistance I had in letting go of life coaching business six years ago, just because my past mentor told me that there's no money in life coaching, gave me the change of direction I needed to get my business to where it is now. And now, I'm bringing everything together – the business experience as well as the mindset experience into a certification that I never imagined was going to happen. So just go with the flow. Allow it. There is no such thing as making mistakes or ruining your business or reputation.

Trust you. Trust that you've got everything you need to make it happen.

As I've said before, your business is a 3D printout of your thoughts. If you don't work on your mindset, nothing is going to grow. If you don't work on what is best for your business, understand that it is an emotional journey, a spiritual journey, you're never going to take your business to the next level, no matter what business you are in. Yes, some people say there's no emotion in business, which I agree with until a certain point. There can be no emotion in ways, however, we are people, and as people we are always going to be

triggered. So, you want to learn to not let your emotion dictate where your business is going and, especially not base your decisions off of fear.

If we are connected to giving, we can impact more people. It's not about me. It's not about you. It's a duty that you have. People will judge you no matter what, so whether you put yourself out there or not, people will still judge you. If you don't do anything, people will judge you because you haven't done anything. If you do something people will judge you because you've done something.

So, the question is, are you going to let other people stop you from achieving your dream because you're afraid of them judging you? Or are you going to step up and do it anyway because they're going to judge you regardless?

Let go of judgement

One of the first things I noticed when I was afraid of people judging me was that I was the first one to judge. I was the first one to judge myself. I was the first one to judge others. I was the first one to be in that position of seeing someone and judging who they are. I was feeling awful about it, even though I would never say it to anybody.

Even if you aren't telling anyone about your judgement, be honest with yourself when you catch yourself doing it. Are you judging others? Are you judging yourself? Have you been tough and judged people doing Facebook Lives – the ones who are actually showing up on social media? Stop judging because they're doing their best and at least they're showing up. What are you doing?

A lot of people don't even know what ego is and it fascinates me. For example, when you decide what car you want to buy, you all of a sudden see it everywhere. This is caused by our reticular activators system in our brain, which pick up the signal that you want to buy the car so it will look for it and will find it everywhere.

Have you experienced this or something similar? When I started personal development, I learned about ego and I started to notice my ego all the time. We all have ego and it's part of us. This is the best way I can explain to you what ego is, ego is a personality that we create from the moment we are born until 7 years old. It's not who you are, it's how you behave. When I started personal development, I knew what ego was and I recognised ego. When we are born till the age of seven, we create a box around us that is actually helping us stay protected. I identify this box as the ego. So, when you are growing up you start to build that protection around you so that you don't die. It's like a survival mechanism.

The question is, when we come up with fears is it really a life or death situation? Because if it isn't, then let it go. And let's lean into it. And so ego is our protector. It is our little voice that tells us don't do that, that's going to be dangerous, you're going hurt yourself. It is coming from experience. But, do you really want your past experience to dictate what your future is going to be? If you talk about someone you like, to someone who is madly in love, they're going to tell you, 'Yeah, of course you want to date that person. Love is amazing'. If you meet someone who has been hurt multiple times in love and you tell them you're falling in love, they're going to tell you to be careful, don't trust anybody, they're only going to cheat on you, and eventually leave you. Ego is that person, depending on your experiences, that is going to make up and decide what your life should be like. And they're going to try to protect you from living the same experience over and over again.

I believe that we are all in a box and the ego put us into this box. And to get out of the box, there are instructions, but instructions are usually attached on the outside of the box. So, no matter how long your neck is, you can't really read what it says on the front of the box. To do that, you need to get a coach, you need to get someone from the outside who can clearly see how you're going to get yourself out. You cannot do it by yourself, you need help, we all do. As a coach, I always suggest to see someone who can really help you a couple times a month to just go through things that are stopping you from reaching the next level. I have had a coach for five years now and I still go, because it has helped me to take the business to a whole new level.

Sometimes, it's also ok to give in to ego if there is no negative repercussion to you. Give your ego some love. Create a balanced mindset between your ego and your higher self. And the more you do it, the more your ego will quieten down.

The art of being centred

To be centred means to be aligned, it doesn't mean to be perfect. Well, I don't believe in balance. A lot of the time people say you need to find a balanced life – that is bullshit. When you have children, everything is about your kids, no matter what you do it revolves around your kids and when you meet someone who has just had a kid, they want to talk to you about kids all the time. When you meet someone who just got a dog, they're going to talk about the dog all the time. Our brain is anxious, and anxious brains always go through patterns, and always bring what we know. So right now, you can only concentrate on one thing at a time. If you have a business, you're going to be obsessed about the business talk. Yes, you can also do other stuff. But what I'm saying is, you need to bring passion to be able to run a business and if you are centred, you're going to be able to do it a lot more. It doesn't need to be balanced, but it does need to be centred.

For me, centred means that you meditate every day, or at least most of the days. And you want to start to find a routine where you are putting yourself into a state of understanding that will benefit your life and business. You get your momentum in the day, but being aligned, being centred for me means that you are connected to your higher self. You connect to a higher spirit.

What is ego and what is your higher self telling you? When making decisions, listen to your higher self and recognise when you're in ego. It's a very fine line. Ego sometimes gives you that butterfly feeling, but then the higher self gives you that stomach feeling so it's sort of similar, very similar. For me, one is in my stomach and one is in my belly. It is that very fine line which makes it hard to recognise which one is which.

Start to listen to these feelings and you might even want to write it down in a journal. Every time you have that feeling think about where it is sitting in your body, and what the outcome was when you made a decision. Later, you might say, 'Oh, that was when I felt that, that probably was ego because it was the wrong thing to do'. However, is it right or wrong?

Everything we do is going to take us to the next level of our life. Everything we do is going to help us to become a better version of ourselves. Everything I've done in my life is a piece of the puzzle, of the greater puzzle of my life. If I didn't make decisions that at the time might have been the wrong decision, I wouldn't be speaking right now, writing my third book and having a multimillion dollar business and travelling the world running retreats and having the time of my life. So, I truly believe that our higher self always has our back no matter what. However, the thing is, it isn't a fast process to learn how to spend most of your time in your higher self. It takes time to learn where you are meant to be in this lifetime.

Surround yourself with people who are more successful than you so you can start learning from them. You can start to recognise how to make a decision, you can start to recognise how to run the business, you can start to see who they hang out with. What's their routine? What do they do every day? What are the non-negotiables for them in their life? What are the standards? What do they settle for? What don't they settle for? It's important to surround yourself with people who are more successful than you in whatever area you want to be better. And it's just priceless because they're going to give you a shortcut on how to do it yourself.

Have you ever asked yourself...

What if I can't control my ego?

Well, we all can. You have a choice. We all have a choice. The thing is, do you allow ego to take over? In the amazing book, *Untethered Soul* by Michael A. Singer, he says, 'If your ego was a friend, would you hang out with him or her?' And the answer usually is no. Our ego sometimes tells us stuff like, you're stupid, you make bad decisions, you did this, you did that and we are so tough on ourselves. But think about it. Would you ever hang out with a friend that treats you like that? Well, if you are, you might need to start to change your friends. But if you aren't, if you wouldn't want to hang out with them, why would you let your brain tell you stuff like that? Why would you let your brain say things that you would never say to a friend? So learning how to control your ego doesn't mean that you're going to become a control freak. We want to start to learn how to be in our higher self.

What if I'm afraid of being me and it's easier to fake it?

There's no other way to be, you need to be yourself because if you pretend to be somebody else for too long, the universe is going to give you a wake-up call somehow. They'll bring you a feather first, then a brick and then the whole bus is going to hit you. So, remember, being yourself is the best way to be. Accept yourself, because if you don't, other people will start to knock you down. And your followers will always see through it and you'll lose them too.

What if I don't like meditation?

Well, you know, I didn't like meditation at first either. Now, I like guided meditation and if you go on YouTube there are thousands and thousands and thousands of meditations. I have found so many that are helpful. For guided, there is Esther Hicks or Deepak Chopra. There are so many people to follow that do meditations and they're free on YouTube, so do some listening.

Here is a top tip: during times of uncertainty, we often get stuck playing in the drama triangle. You probably aren't even aware you are playing in it too. The drama triangle consists of three players: the victim, the rescuer and the prosecutor. The victim always believes bad situations are happening to them and they always need a rescuer to help them get out of this situation. The rescuer tries to help the victim out of the negative situation, which enforces the victim mentality. This person is often a family member or a friend. The persecutor pushes someone to become a victim by attacking them – and same with the rescuer. To get out of this triangle, you must stop reacting to each situation and enabling each role. I have played my fair share in the drama triangle and now that I am aware of this, whenever I notice myself contributing, I stop and I apologise for my actions and for participating. Remember, you only need one person to stop playing the game for all the roles to crumble.

The three actions you're going to take from this chapter are:

1. Look for a mindset coach. Find one that can help you to get rid of your limiting beliefs.

_____
_____
_____
_____
_____
_____
_____
_____

2. Have a buddy that is more successful than you in what you want to achieve and be open with them and share your limiting beliefs as well as your wins.

_____
_____
_____
_____
_____
_____
_____
_____

3. Give meditation a go as a way to tune in and listen to your higher self. This can be especially helpful before events or when an important decision needs to be made.

_____
_____
_____
_____
_____
_____
_____
_____

CHAPTER 12

GROW A CULTURE AND A LEGACY

'If you're going to live, leave a legacy. Make a mark on the world that can't be erased.'

–Maya Angelou

Do you want to be a manager or a business owner? Two different things, right?

Well I realised that in business there are different layers of business owners:

- Wannapreneur
- Solopreneur
- Entrepreneur
- Teampreneur
- Soulpreneur

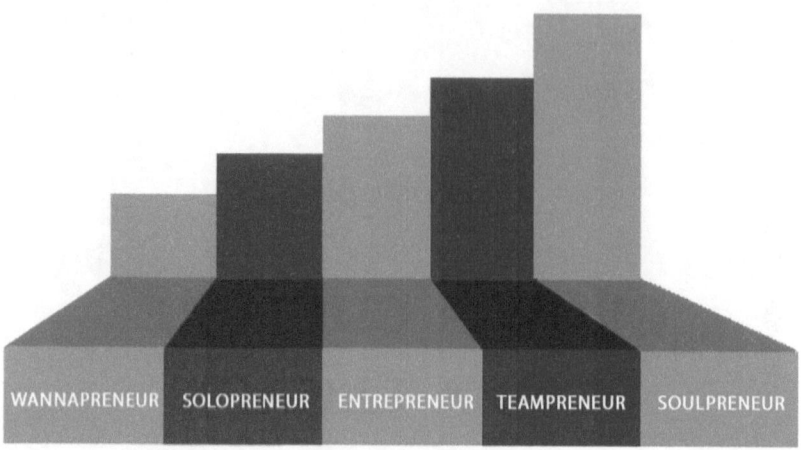

Wannapreneur is that person that wants to be a business owner, but they are too scared to take the leap, so they still have a job and can't get the courage to just do it.

Solopreneur is that person who creates a job for themselves. They work hard for their money and are stuck delivering value to their clients which they can't scale. They can't move it to the next level.

Entrepreneur is a money-making machine. They start to get amazing ideas on how to leverage time to make more money. They help a lot of people, have a successful business and have contractors working for them. They have found a way to truly leverage from being an expert in their niche and have been able to gain a massive following.

Teampreneur is someone who now has a team of people working for them. They can delegate tasks and work to other team members. However, the team members keep leaving because they don't feel the love.

Soulpreneur is someone who has gone through all the above and learned that if you aren't following the passion in your heart, then you are not going to get anywhere in the long term.

Life is about balancing the love and passion with business. And when you run your business from your soul you can then leave a legacy.

I have been through all levels and after years of running my business I found myself getting stuck managing 10 people, plus contractors and solving problems and answering questions all day. It was quite devastating and exhausting.

I used to be a teampreneur and I didn't like it but I didn't know how to change it. I had amazing team members and I could delegate work to them and they were able to get the job done, but after a little bit – a few months to a year – they would leave. I couldn't figure out why! This goes back to how to treat your team members. They need to feel empowered about themselves to do their work properly. If they make a mistake you need to have faith they won't make it again, that they will learn from it. It took time for me to grasp this, and after rotating through staff members, I became drained and felt defeated.

I woke up one morning thinking, *Hold on, this is not what I signed up for!*

I went from marketing, Facebook, Meetup and everything I love, to customer service meetings, finance meetings and dealing with the emotional up and downs of what my clients were going through and all the emotional problems from my team. And I'm like, *No, no, no, no, this is not why I started a business. I wanted to have fun. I wanted to have lifestyle, I wanted freedom!!! And now I'm stuck dealing with problems all day!!!*

I had to learn the hard way. But I finally got it, I had to learn to be a greater leader to leave a lasting legacy.

I had to learn that I can't do it all by myself. At the beginning, I really wanted to do it all on my own. I thought that doing it myself was faster and better than getting someone else to do it. I wanted to be in control of everything. So, if people were doing stuff, I wouldn't trust them, I would control them, I would ask them 1000 times and that would not make them feel empowered.

Delegating is freedom. But you have to learn how to delegate properly so you can actually build that freedom into your life and not have to do it all. As business owners, when we start out, we know we have to wear different hats and do different things. But as the business grows, it can get too much and delegating to other people lightens the load. It's important to manage and know what others are doing for you, but resist the temptation to step in and do it for them.

When I became comfortable with delegating, I took it to the other extreme and started to throw tasks at people expecting them to do them in a day, I used to forget to check and assume they did it all, to find out later that nothing was done!!!

I now know that I first need to set my expectation, give a time frame, create a procedure and follow-up to ensure the project is in progress and in the direction I wanted it to go.

Cultures keep the business afloat, and if your clients are not happy, if your team is not happy, if your contractors are not happy, you're not going to be successful in business. So, it's about supporting them to find the best way for them to make things work.

For your clients, team and contractors to thrive and succeed, they need your support.

It's about building a five-star culture.

I introduced the five-star service to our business, so everyone in the team had a #fmfivestar and every time they did something outstanding they would put a #fmfivestar, which would make me happy and it would make them proud to be a part of a five-star service in my business. They were proud of helping the clients five-star, they were proud to help each other as a five-star. It's one way to show how much people really care and how proud they are to give their best service.

Treat your team as if they are your clients, not as if they are your family. Love them like a family, but don't treat them like your family. Sometimes we can be guilty of treating our family not that nice, so treating them like a client will make you want to treat them kindly and give love, but also hold them accountable and give them some tough love when they need it. But always make sure that they can come to you, they can talk to you and you provide support.

What is the culture?

For us at Empowering Events, culture is all being on the same page about our values and our goals.

The only way to grow a culture is to keep changing and evolving your brain to ensure you leave the legacy you want. You will not be able to grow or get to your next destination if you don't learn to change and adapt to situations. As you have probably noticed, throughout each stage from invisible to invincible you must always take risks. You must take risks to evolve to the next step to get to the next level.

So, how do you take risks without losing it all? Well firstly, you have to be okay with losing what you've created. In business, commitment and taking risks are important factors, not just the ability to commit financially. I'm sure you have made a decision in the past that was risky, but you just let it flow. I'm sure there was a time you didn't overthink it and you just put your whole heart into it and jumped right in. The worst-case scenario is not getting the best-case scenario.

I wasn't always able to think like this. As you know, I had to work on my mindset. So how exactly do you get the right mindset in business so that you are okay with taking risks?

You need to believe that what you want to be is what you will be. Think positive and the universe will bring positivity your way. There will be challenges with every risk you take, but these challenges will just help you grow and become a better leader and a better person. This is how you keep growing and evolving and this is how you can keep your legacy alive. I'm not saying to go and risk everything because you do have to think strategically about your business.

Think about the various outcomes that could come from making a risky decision. If you take a risk and it doesn't work out the way you planned it would, you need to be prepared to learn from it to survive in difficult situations. You need to learn how to adapt when your business isn't at its high. What is your backup plan? Because business is not just about your gut feeling. It can be taking one step at a time in order to see the bigger picture and what you want your vision to be. You need to plan the different aspects in business – even the smallest and simplest ones.

Learn to take risks and be okay with stepping into the unknown. Let's be grateful about the decisions you've made so far because it brought you to where you currently are. Make decisions for your future self, and not for your current self. And this is how you can start to work towards your legacy.

What is leaving a legacy?

Your legacy can be empowering your team to take care of the business without you having to micromanage them. It is knowing that things are going to continue happening and things are going to keep moving ahead. You want to start to put systems in place and if that's not your strength, get someone to help you, even as a contractor, to help you put systems in place. I've learned so much from other contractors and people who help us that now it has started to become my strength.

Put systems in place that everybody can follow. Most business owners opt to put systems in place before they hire people. But, you can always hire people first, then let them put the systems in place once they have been instructed in what to do and understand your expectations. This saves you time, and helps them become an expert in your business. If you don't have systems in place, the team can create them for you. So, don't wait until everything is perfect, but find people and build systems together.

Choose your business values together and let your team be part of that. Let your team understand and agree what the values are in the business and what you stand for.

Let go of perfectionism: it's not going to be perfect. Starting something is better than not doing anything. Stop wanting to do it all by yourself, let others chip in or do it for you. Let them make mistakes so they can learn and become independent.

Have you ever asked yourself…

What if I choose the wrong team member?

Well, you will. And you will learn how to choose the right person for the team. And making mistakes will actually help you to get clear about what type of business you want to run and what type of people you want to have around you. I used to choose people like me because I like them the most and I wanted to be around them. But the thing is, there is really only one of me. I don't need someone else's creativity. I need someone that can do stuff. That can start and finish a project. I used to hire people that were all like me – starters. They love starting stuff, but they don't love to implement or finish it. These days I look to complement my strengths and weaknesses rather than matching them.

What if I find the right person and they leave me?

They will! They will definitely leave you so don't be afraid of that, let that go as well. Your goal is to make this person a better person and if they leave and go on to do what they dream, then you have done your job. They will move on and when it's time, it's usually best for you, the business and for them. So don't be afraid and don't try to hold onto people because, as Tony Robbins says, 'It is not who you hired that can destroy your business, but who you fail to fire'.

Understand that people will come and go. People will leave if they don't feel right. At first, every time someone who had a major role in the team left, it made me feel terrified – but I've since learned that was when the business usually took a whole new turn and jumped to the next level.

How can I leave a legacy?

Being in business is about paying it forward. Pay it forward for yourself, for your team, for your clients, for your Marias – for the world. It's your business and you can leave a legacy that creates ripple effects that last a lifetime. So, pay it forward and don't be greedy along the way. Be generous. You will notice the more generous you are, the more people will want to buy from you and the more people will want to work with you. Trust me, I have done events where only one person has shown up, but I didn't let that stop me. Instead, I learned from that and I grew from it and I was able to learn to take risks from that – and now I have hosted events and workshops with hundreds of people. One thing I really learned, is to stay in your heart, give as much as you can, build the quantity of your clients and the quality will come.

Be close with your audience, to your clients, so you understand what they need, so you can help them get to the next level, as well as you. You cannot do it the other way around. Be with them and you will be okay. You want to experience, feel and get to know your clients properly. This shouldn't be a chore, you should genuinely want to do this. Sometimes, you have to go through the time wasters to get to the right people you want to work with. Put your time in and the ripple effects that will come from that will be unbelievable.

I hope my legacy will create a positive and lasting ripple effect across the world. I want to help as many people as I can and I want the world to become a better place because of it. Remember, you are in business to create positive change, so take that risk, take that leap of faith and work your way towards invincible so you can help even more people.

The three actions you're going to take from this chapter are:

1. Do it yesterday! Hire someone. Delegate all the things that you don't like. For example, get a chef, get a cleaner, get a laundry person. I even got a person my car, I've got everything sorted because my time is way more valuable spent in what I'm good at instead of wasting time in things that I don't like doing.

_____
_____
_____
_____
_____
_____
_____

2. Work together with your team to build systems by recording training while you train them, then having them write the procedures up.

_____
_____
_____
_____
_____
_____
_____

3. Start using Asana to assign tasks to your team. I love Asana, it has been helping me so much in the business and has been taking everything to the next level. So just go and do it!

_____
_____
_____
_____
_____
_____
_____

AFTERWORD

As I am writing this, I feel very fortunate to be able to write my third book – an accomplishment many strive for and I do not take this for granted.

I have spent three years, and countless hours, working towards becoming invincible in every area of my life. I am proud of the decisions I have made along the way to get to where I am.

It's crazy, every year I invested in my brain, in growing and becoming a better version of myself.

There is always room to grow. There is always room to learn. There is always room to take another step. So, don't wait. Take action now. Take action towards being invincible. Whether in your business or in your personal life, continue to reach to become a better version of yourself. Once you start to do this, you can truly start helping more people.

I hope this book has helped you realise the impact you can make on this world. The more invincible you are, the more impact you can make. As you work through my strategies, keep that in mind. If you find yourself going through hard times, remember the reason you started your business. Remember why you wanted to help people. Your business is a 3D printout of your thoughts, so cherish and take care of your thoughts and watch your business go to the next level.

Don't give up when your business is going through a rough patch. Keep pushing through and challenging yourself to think outside of the box. Use my strategies to guide you but put your own spin on them. Do what works best for you.

Let's all work together to create a lasting, positive impact on this world.

ABOUT THE AUTHOR

After arriving in Australia from Italy 11 years ago, Francesca Moi has successfully created a business which allows entrepreneurs to collaborate and celebrate each other while living their passion. She is the perfect example of how a mindset can transform your business and become something greater than yourself.

Francesca started her journey by moving across the world with the dream of becoming a successful life coach. But soon after arriving, she realised the market was saturated and that her dream was slipping away.

Not one to turn down a challenge, Francesca studied other successful entrepreneurs to discover what made them tick and learn the pattern, or formula for success. A journey that took her to the stage where she learned that to become successful, she would have to adopt, not only the right mindset, but also strategies that involved an on and offline presence. Within three months of implementing these strategies she became fully booked as a 1:1 life coach, but there was something inside her that wanted to strive further, to have a greater impact on others. It wasn't until a life coach approached her and asked how she became fully booked, and then another and another, that Francesca saw the opportunity to expand her own business, while also helping others to do the same.

She created Academy Family, a program that helps entrepreneurs, business owners, speakers and coaches step up and fulfil their passion using the same strategies that Francesca used herself. As time went on, she perfected and elevated these strategies, continually growing and serving her clients so they can grow too, teaching them how to go from invisible to invincible on and offline. Francesca is extremely passionate about using events and social media to raise her client's profiles and create one-to-many businesses, rather than slaving away in a one on one and time-for-money business that they're unable to scale. In three and a half years she has created a million-dollar business that serves a community of 250 entrepreneurs to support and transform alongside one another.

About The Author

Francesca has continued to step up and show up for her clients with her infectious personality, by going WORLDWIDE, allowing her to generate a community of entrepreneurs who passionately live life on their terms, while generating an income.

Francesca's Website:

www.empoweringevents.com.au
francescamoi.com
www.instagram.com/FrancescaMoiFM
https://www.facebook.com/francesca.moi

Email: marketing@empoweringevents.com.au

HIRE A VA

Empower Your Business with Francesca Moi

Ready to kick your business into high gear and finally master that elusive art of delegation and time management? Let's make it happen together! I'm Francesca Moi, and I'm thrilled to introduce you to my Virtual Assistant Agency, Empowering Virtual Solution. This isn't just about getting things off your plate; it's about transforming how your business operates.

Imagine having a team of expertly trained Virtual Assistants who handle your day-to-day tasks, freeing you up to focus on big-picture strategies and growth. That's what hundreds of entrepreneurs have achieved working with us, and now it's your turn. Dive into a world where your business runs smoother, grows faster, and feels a whole lot easier to manage.

Join our community of go-getters who've transformed their businesses with a little help from their dedicated virtual teams. It's time to empower your business dreams with real solutions. Let's get started and watch your business soar!

Are you...

- Not having enough time to manage your Social Media?
- Not having enough time to repurpose your content on Facebook and generate more leads?
- Feeling like admin tasks are piling up and taking you away from what you do best?
- Having a hard time with technology and wishing there was someone there that could work it all out for you?

If you've answered YES to one of the questions above, I GET YOU!

We've all been there, working tirelessly for hours and feeling like you are not getting enough done.

Time is never enough, and it's even harder if we don't have anyone cheering us, supporting us, and working it all out for us! You end up feeling stuck and frustrated. You have big dreams and many ideas, and you want to help more and more people, but you don't have the time or energy to scale your business and match your BIG aspirations!

This is the reason why **Empowering Virtual Solution** came to life.

This VA program is for time-poor business owners who need a set of helping hands in their business to gain more time and focus more on their zone of genius rather than drowning in doing all things IN their business.

Our team has helped over 100 business owners get their lives back whilst achieving all of their business and personal goals. We've trained and supplied over 100 VAs and taught them strategies to achieve the outcome that you want faster and more effectively.

Introduction to Empowering Virtual Solution

Empowering Virtual Solution Ltd Pty is an Australian outsourcing agency that seamlessly connects your business with skilled Virtual Assistants (VAs) from the Philippines. We manage the entire process, including:

- Hiring
- Training
- Project Management
- HR & Payroll
- Disruption/Replacement Cover

Our Unique Approach:
Our support goes beyond matching you with a VA. We provide continuous assistance through an experienced supervisor, help assign tasks to maximise efficiency, and offer access to business coaching and a supportive community of business owners.

Our Process:
To join our team, VAs must:

- Be highly motivated and committed
- Pass a stringent application process
- Complete our specialised training
- Have an approved home workspace

How We Match:
Personality Test: We require a personality test from you to ensure a compatible match.
Skills Assessment: We match VAs based on the specific skills you need.

Your VA is specifically trained in the below Programs:
- Marketing
- Social Media
- Administrative Tasks
- Customer Service Tasks
- Customer Relationship Management

Industries We Serve:

Our VAs are effectively working and driving success in various industries, such as:

- Legal & Immigration
- Real Estate & Construction
- Health & Wellness
- Travel Agencies
- Education & Coaching
- Financial Services & Accounting
- Software & IT
- Marketing & Advertising
- E-Commerce & Retail

Our VAs are integral to the daily operations and growth of businesses across these sectors. They ensure efficiency and allow business owners to focus on strategic initiatives.

OUR PACKAGES:
FULL TIME VA: 40-Hours work week
PART TIME VA: 20-Hours work week

CONTACT THE TEAM
Get started with your VA Now! Contact us to learn more! Scan this code:

HIRE A VA

DON'T MISS OUT!!

BUMS ON SEATS

THE POWER OF DELEGATION

FOLLOW ME - SHUTTUPP

AVAILABLE BOOKS

SCAN THE CODE TO LEARN MORE

NOTES

www.ingramcontent.com/pod-product-compliance
Lightning Source LLC
Chambersburg PA
CBHW021147080526
44588CB00008B/249